What Others are Saying About

RealTime
Coaching

How to Make the Minute-by-Minute Decisions
That Unleash the Power in Your People

"The approach fills a gap in published business theory by tackling, in a practical way, the 'last three feet' of management. It embraces the all-important emotional underpinnings of 'doing' rather than just the intellectual basis of 'planning to do.' "
> **Charles A. Dowd, President**
> **Delta Faucet Co.**

"RealTime Coaching provides a very common sense approach to coaching that does a much better job of encouraging employee accountability for their performance than other books I've read. I will encourage my management team to use this book as a resource."
> **Donald W. Hecht, Director of Sales and Marketing**
> **Elanco Animal Health, Division of Eli Lilly & Company**

"Ron Ernst's RealTime Coaching is a breakthrough how-to book! The theory and practice of coaching are laid out in a pragmatic, easy-to-learn fashion. Excellent real life examples and scenarios. If you learn one new skill this business year, learn coaching via RealTime Coaching!"
> **Terry Reilly, Partner**
> **J.D. Powers and Associates**

"I would highly recommend this book to any mid-level manager or executive as a concise, cohesive presentation of coaching. It is structured for quick reading, and it is formatted the way reality presents itself—directly and rapidly. I would also give it to my direct reports to read, and then we'd cut the time needed for excellent coaching outcomes in half."
Dale Mowry, Vice President Broadcast Systems Division
Harris Corporation

"Every manager who wants to improve his/her relationship with persons reporting to them should read this book to become a more effective coach - the only style of management that produces quality. Send me a case of books - they will make great reading prior to next planning session."
Larry J. Hannah, President, U.S. Operations
Harlan Sprague Dowley, Inc.

"Finally, a book with more than theory. A book that demonstrates the implementation process. A book that should be in the hands of every manager, boss, supervisor, and leader."
Connie Dillman, Chief Operating Officer
Noble of Indiana, Inc.

"Okay, so we now know that we should all be coaches. But what exactly does that mean and how do we go about it? Ron Ernst's gem of a book is the next best thing to having your own personal executive coach in the learning process."
Ed Engledow, President
Engledow Group

"Very good book. It really shows the need to ask employees to self-evaluate rather than the boss always doing the evaluation. I'm sure I'll refer back to the planning guide often."
Rich Westlake, Managing Member
Hansen & Horn Group II, LLC.

"Too often 'management' books are long on theory and short on application. Thanks for writing a book that can be used as a 'field manual' to more effective leadership. Every new supervisor should be issued a copy of your book!"
Frank Pianki, Assistant Professor of Business
Anderson University

"Wow! A refreshing look at leadership for the new millennium. Ron has done a superb job of creating a practical guide for leadership development. A must read for anyone who wishes to become an 'effective' leader."

Steven P. Osborn, President
C E Solutions, Inc.

"This is truly the first book that doesn't just tell me I have to fix my problems, but gets to the practical how to fix them. It's time for RealTime Coaching! We must change our approach to leading and not herding or forcing employees to follow us. Leading by listening and coaching is the only way to take on the challenge of quality and growth."

Mike Bursaw, President
Crown Point Graphics, Inc.

Published by:
Leadership Horizons, LLC
301 E. Carmel Drive, Suite D 500
Carmel, IN 46032-4812
317-844-5587
Toll free 1-888-262-2477
Fax 317-581-9226

First printing, January 1999
Second printing, June 1999
Third printing, June 2000
Fourth printing, June 2001

Design by Willow Marketing, Indianapolis, IN
Printed in the United States of America

Library of Congress Catalog Card Number: 98-96833

Ernst, Ronald L.
    RealTime Coaching: How to make the minute-by-minute decisions that unleash the power in your people.

ISBN: 0-9668868-0-1

RealTime
Coaching

How to Make the Minute-by-Minute Decisions
That Unleash the Power in Your People

Ron Ernst • President
Leadership Horizons, LLC

Leadership Horizons, LLC
301 E. Carmel Drive, Suite D 500 • Carmel, IN 46032-4812
(317)844-5587 • Fax (317)581-9226
ron@leadershiphorizons.com

To My Coaches

— To my wife and personal coach for support, encouragement, and unconditional love. Thank you, Carol.

— To my boys, Boyd and Blake, who always have a way of testing my coaching abilities and in the process making me a better coach. Thanks, guys.

— To Dr. William Glasser for his brilliance in helping us all better understand "why we do what we do."

— To Dr. Robert Wubbolding for his clarity of thought, creativity and passion for his profession.

— To Bill Bonstetter for pioneering practical ways to use the knowledge of values and behavior in creating more effective and enjoyable personal and professional relationships.

— To Marlene Elliott, a true coach's coach, for her inspiration and unwavering commitment to my success.

— To Robert Alderman who pushed me to examine how my theoretical value was being satisfied and in the process encouraged the completion of *RealTime Coaching*.

— To Willow Marketing for their extraordinary effort in designing a reader-friendly book.

— To Ken Honeywell, my editor, for helping me organize my thoughts into a coherent message.

— To all my clients and friends who reviewed my manuscript, gave me their thoughts and helped me better understand the coaching process.

Foreword

Scan the Business section of any library or bookstore today (or attend a management seminar), and you'll find literally hundreds of books designed to motivate you, teach you better management skills, and make you a more effective boss. Scan the Self-Help section (or hire a consultant or psychologist), and you'll find all sorts of "personality profiles" that arrange people into categories according to what they believe or the way they behave.

What you'll find is, most management books are long on hyperbole and short on practical methods for really improving the quality of communications in your place of business. At the same time, most methods of personality profiling paint a nice picture of the "type of person" you are and leave it at that, which can lead to a mentality that says, "This is just who I am, and you have to deal with me."

Ron Ernst's *RealTime Coaching* is different. Truly different. It's not just a list of platitudes or suggestions, but a well-developed system for bringing out the best in your employees, every minute of every day.

Why does *RealTime Coaching* work? It works because Ron based his approach to coaching on a scientific, accepted model of what motivates people and why different people behave in different ways. Once you experience *RealTime Coaching*, you'll never again be stuck for a way to resolve difficult situations in your organization.

Even more important, *RealTime Coaching* doesn't merely place people in categories you have to react to. It uses the DISC language as a basis for adapting your own behavior to the situations you encounter at work...and influencing employees to adapt their own behavior to align their personal desires with the goals and objectives of the organization.

In truth, I suspect you'll find *RealTime Coaching* to be of bene-fit to you not only in your workplace, but in your communications with your spouse, your friends, your family, and everyone else in your life. It's a powerful tool for smarter, better communication that really gets results. I encourage you to put *RealTime Coaching* to work for you now!

Bill J. Bonnstetter
President and Founder
TTI Performance Systems, Ltd.

Preface

In retrospect, I began using the coaching dialogue you're about to learn in the mid 1970s. At the time, I had just received an MBA from The Ohio State University and was employed as a management consultant. My duties included research and analysis, strategic planning, report writing, client presentations, and conducting a fair amount of stand-up management training. It was this last responsibility that challenged what I knew about people. It wasn't the presentations that concerned me–I was a far better than average presenter–it was the person who worked for me. I was, you see, a *boss* for the first time in my life! Judy (not her real name) was assigned to me. It was my responsibility to develop Judy in the art and science of management training. And I wasn't making much progress.

After several months of practice, Judy just wasn't getting it–and she knew it. Her presentation style was stilted, she'd get lost in her presentation, and the audience groaned at her attempts at humor. As a result, her self-confidence was falling sharply. My attempts at advice–"Here try this" or "Present it this way"–were to no avail. I had to try something different.

After a particularly trying presentation we had a brief break. We walked to the lobby of the hotel where we were presenting and sat down. I knew another pep talk would seem laughably superficial. After a rather long silence, I turned to Judy. Her face showed all the frustration and pain of months of agonizing trials. "Judy," I began, "Do you want to be a trainer?" She thought for a brief moment, then stated, very firmly, "Yes, I really do." I replied to her, with what, in retrospect, was a gridlock-breaking question, "Then what do you need from me? How can I help?"

The ensuing conversation was a turning point for both of us.

Judy began to ask questions about how I presented, how I prepared, what I thought about during a presentation, and how I gauged time so we ended on schedule. I began to understand more about myself–that I was critiquing her presentations and offering my advice from the perspective of what *I* thought she needed to know, not what *she* wanted to learn.

I also realized that people have a natural tendency to discount the unique gifts and talents they bring to their jobs. In our conversation, Judy began relating personal stories that were rich in illustrating the concepts she was presenting, but she was afraid to use them because she thought they were "self-promoting" and "inappropriate." I encouraged her to bring more of her personal self to her presentation and to take off the artificial mask she felt she needed to hide behind. The result was instantaneous. Her comfort level increased, her presentations flowed, and the audience was now fully engaged with her.

This experience revealed to me the power that lies within people if we only know how to unleash it. *RealTime Coaching* is my contribution to all *bosses* who want to make the minute-by-minute decisions that unleash the power in the people they manage. Encourage them to take off their masks and share with you what they really want from their jobs and from you. Value the unique gifts and contributions each person brings to the job. And then watch as people naturally take your organization to new heights.

Enjoy!

Ron Ernst
January 1, 1999
Tee Lake
Lewiston, Michigan

Table of Contents

Introduction

Why RealTime Coaching?

The "last three feet" between two people is the most overlooked part of leadership training. What is said, or left unsaid, determines the effectiveness of the leader and the commitment of the follower.

Knowledge, in the absence of theory, is useless. Knowledge is prediction, and knowledge comes from theory. Experience teaches nothing without theory. Do not try to copy someone else's success. Unless you understand the theory behind it, trying to copy it can lead to complete chaos.

—W. Edwards Deming

RealTime Coaching is written for practitioners: managers, executives, and leaders who day-to-day, minute-by-minute, are trying to accomplish their organizational goals with and through people.

Coaching is a new way of relating with those you work with and can pay extraordinary dividends in improved performance, increased productivity, and loyalty to you and your organization. As a manager of people, the more you are viewed as someone interested in helping other people get what *they* want, the more your position as a leader will be assured. But, you may be asking, "Why *coaching* and why *now?*"

Technology Up, Employee Productivity Flat

Organizations today have access to more technology than ever before in the history of American business. Businesses, even the smallest ones, have opportunities to market their products and services around the world; in fact, the Internet can expose a company to a worldwide audience literally at the touch of a button.

And the Internet, of course, is just the latest in a long line of technological breakthroughs that have radically changed the way we do business. Remember when cellular phones were such a luxury that some enterprising entrepreneurs were marketing fake phones? In 1983, there were no cellular phone users at all. In 1990, there were about 5.3 million cellular phone users. By 1995, there were nearly 33.8 million and many of the phones they used were given to them free of charge!

Other technologies have grown in similarly dramatic fashion. In 1985, there were just over 12 million PCs in use. In 1993, there were more than 14.8 million PCs *sold*. In 1982, there were only 32,000 industrial robots in use; by 1995, that number had jumped to more than 20 million!

Put it this way: if automotive technology advanced at the same rate as computer technology, you'd be able to buy a Lexus today for $2.00. Your new luxury car would travel at the speed of sound and get about 600 miles to the thimbleful of gas!

Desktop and laptop computers, fax machines, wireless voice and now wireless data services, voice mail, and robots all have come to prominence in the last 15 years. All have added new opportunities to work faster, smarter, and more productively. The question is, has business taken advantage of these opportunities?

The answer, perhaps surprisingly, is no. Quite the contrary: studies have suggested that technology has not resulted in an increase in productivity.

American worker productivity (output per worker hour) has risen just 1.2% per year between 1979 and 1994. Compare this with the average 3.4% per year productivity gain in the postwar years. Is it a coincidence that the fall off in productivity coincides with the rise of technology in the workplace?

Figure 1

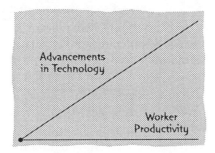

Advancements in Technology Compared
to Increases in Worker Productivity

This point is graphically illustrated in Figure 1. While technology—by any measure—has advanced along an extraordinarily steep incline in the past 25 years, worker productivity has barely moved at all. The fact is, advancements in technology have not resulted in improvements in productivity. Why?

I think there are several reasons:

- Over reliance on analyzing and planning "*what* to do" at the expense of implementing (or coaching) "*how* to do it."

- Hierarchically based relationships between managers and employees that breed fear and resentment, not creativity and empowerment.

- Hiring practices and management promotion decisions that *mismatch* people with jobs.

Not coincidentally, these are exactly the challenges *RealTime Coaching* addresses. *RealTime Coaching* is the missing link between setting corporate goals, and achieving them, with and through other people. It's a proven way to influence, manage, and motivate people to perform at their absolute best.

How This Book Is Different

I started my career in traditional management consulting, spending eleven years honing my "hard side" skills of analysis, problem solving, and planning. I soon realized that corporate performance requires leaders to blend their "hard side" business skills with their "soft side" skills of building effective human relations. I also noticed an imbalance—that most managers were far better trained and more experienced in using their hard side analytical skills than in their softer "people" skills. The need, I concluded, to develop coaching skills was great. So I began investigating to find a process that would help managers become better coaches.

But most books I found on coaching fell short in several ways. Few provided a theory of how the mind works. Most did not even demonstrate the coaching dialogue, and none effectively bridged the gap between theory and application. It was not until I discovered a practical theory of how the human mind works that the pieces started falling into place. The result is *RealTime Coaching*, a pragmatic and actionable integration of hard nosed management planning and the psychology of human behavior. You'll find *RealTime Coaching* a practical, theory-based, and richly illustrated book that helps you become a better coach.

RealTime Coaching is unique for three very important reasons:

1. *It's based on a theory of human behavior.* As Deming states in the quote at the start of this introduction, "Knowledge in the absence of theory is useless." Many books on coaching and leadership are chock-full of sports analogies and interesting anecdotes and present memorable acronyms, but none are based on a theory of how the human mind works.

   In *RealTime Coaching*, we've drawn on the concepts of Choice Theory developed by Dr. William Glasser. The result is an approach based on a solid, jargon-free, and easy-to-understand theory of human behavior.

   We'll use these concepts so you can better understand human behavior: what motivates people and why they do what they do. That's why *RealTime Coaching* starts not with application but with theory. In Chapters 3–6, we'll be developing a model of human behavior that will serve as your road map. It goes like this:

- All people (including you) go to work because they *want* something. We'll find that these wants, while unique to each of us, are rooted in six basic values. We'll also discover that people see the world around them through their basic values. In other words, the results they achieve from their behaviors are perceived through personal and unique filters that assign a meaning or value to the results.

- The *motivation* for all behavior is the energy created within people when they become aware that what they perceive they're getting does not match what they really want. The greater the mismatch (and the greater the pain), the higher the motivation. And, while people are essentially in control of motivating themselves, managers can influence employees by understanding the values that motivate them.

- During the work day, we use *specific behaviors* to obtain what we want. In *RealTime Coaching*, you'll learn about the four basic behavioral styles and how people use them to try to satisfy their desires. You'll see how these core behavior styles differ greatly from one another, and how you can adjust your own communication style to more effectively help your employees satisfy their own needs and the needs of the organization.

- If you want something other than what you're getting, you have to *change* either your behavior or your goal. Too often, an employee who is frustrated in getting his or her needs met is stuck in a cycle of doing the same thing over and over again. Through *RealTime Coaching*, you'll be able to help employees realize why they're stuck and help them come up with solid strategies for change that get them where they want to go.

2. *The coaching process is demonstrated.* An effective way for you to learn the coaching process is to observe the skill in use. Nearly forty percent of this book is devoted to dialogues between coaches and employees. Demonstrations present a variety of situations and illustrate the *RealTime Coaching* model in action.

The Four Principles of *RealTime Coaching* (which you will learn in Chapters 3–6) are the foundation for our coaching model. The process is then demonstrated in Chapters 8–11. The actual coaching process is a dialogue, based on a cluster of questions the coach asks, all rooted in these principles. The goal of the process is to:

- Encourage employees to critically self-evaluate whether their chosen behaviors are getting them what they want.

- Explore what employees want from their jobs, their co-workers, you, and others, and the human relationships necessary to get what they want.

- Ask employees to precisely identify the behavior they are using to get what they want, and the effect of that behavior on others.

- Help employees, collaboratively with the coach, develop a specific plan of action that will get them more of what they and the organization want.

3. *Commentary within each coaching demonstration links theory and application.* A unique addition called Coach's Thoughts is written into each dialogue. You can "eavesdrop" on the real-time thinking process of the coach to

better understand how the theory is linked to application.

Chapters 8–11, the Coaching Dialogues, provide several coaching demonstrations. These demonstrations allow you to study *RealTime Coaching* in action. Finally, Chapter 12 will help you get started on your own program to develop your coaching skills.

RealTime Coaching works. I've seen it applied successfully in literally hundreds of cases. On the following pages you'll learn the difference between planning and implementation, why people behave the way they do, and how to make the minute-by-minute— *real time*— decisions that unleash the power of your people.

8

Chapter 1

Our Strategy is Brilliant!

So Why is Our Organization Struggling?

Empowerment is not the things you do to or for people, it's the impediments you take away, leaving space for folks to empower themselves.

— Terry Neill, Managing Partner
Worldwide Change Practice
Andersen Consulting

Change is a door that can be opened only from the inside.

Do any of following situations sound familiar?

We have all these planning meetings, review mounds of research, have endless discussions, and finally agree on a plan. And then nothing happens. Absolutely nothing. We just keeping doing the same thing. Oh, we still talk about it a lot, but in reality nothing has changed.

Boy, this would be a great team if only Pat would cooperate more. Always disagreeing, often late for meetings, seldom prepared for our discussions. I don't know why we put up with him.

We've got to improve. Our TQM program is brilliant. I don't know why the plant people aren't embracing it. Can't they see their jobs are at stake?

*We're just not as sharp as we used to be. Oh, we're prof-
itable, but new ideas are scarce to nonexistent. I'm really
nervous about the future and our ability to compete.*

*I don't know what's gotten into Denise. She used to be one
of our top performers. Now all I hear about is how irritable
and argumentative she is. I just don't know how to handle
her.*

*Larry has been with us since the start. A brilliant chief
financial officer—creative, competent, loyal. But don't cross
him. I mean, whoa, the public scathings, the sharp criti-
cisms. His right-hand accountant quit and called him "the
most arrogant SOB I've ever met!" For the good of the company, I can't let this continue.*

Or, as one of my clients put it, "Our strategy is brilliant! So
why is our organization struggling?"

The Real Problem Is Not The Strategy

I had what most would call a traditional business school education: a BS in marketing and an MBA from Big Ten universities. I
felt as prepared as any of my classmates to enter the business
world. We were all well versed in the "hard side" of business:
accounting, marketing, production, finance, quantitative analysis,
and strategy development. In fact, strategic planning was taught as
the key to a successful organization, and the concept appealed
strongly to me. As a result, my first job was with a management
consulting firm. I felt confident that what they taught me in B-
school—analysis, problem solving, and planning—I could do for
our clients. And I did.

Research was our firm's forte. We conducted hundreds of studies for clients around the globe. I was on a first-name basis with
most airline reservations agents. We prepared mounds of data,
synthesized facts from a variety of sources, and wrote volumes of
reports, all neatly presented in three-ring binders. Our clients
loved it (or so I thought) and they usually paid our invoices.

But a funny thing started to happen. I began to sense that,

while our reports were truly impressive, I doubted whether many of our clients actually implemented our recommendations. Despite my youth, I was even so brash to ask them, "Did you get what you wanted from us?"

"Yes," most of them said (Whew!), "but...we didn't get what we really needed." I felt more than once that I was on thin ice here.

"What do you mean?" I asked in my best MBA tone.

"Well," they said, "the real problem is not our strategy." Now they tell me, I thought. Could it have been possible that everything I was taught in business school was not the solution?

Yes. I came to realize that my clients were right. They recognized problems. They wanted to change. But most attempts to implement change within an organization fail or at least don't deliver the desired results. Why? Because during implementation, the desire to maintain the status quo is usually far stronger than any attempts to change. (I found out later that organizational psychologists call this *homeostasis*.[1] Kind of like one of Newton's laws — an organization not improving will tend to not improve itself out of existence rather than change.)

Change, if achieved, comes with an emotional cost: stress, fear, tension, and anxiety. When these human emotions are ignored, they can sabotage the best executive's attempts at improvement.

Total Quality Management (TQM) is an excellent example of good intentions gone awry that illustrates this point. TQM started out on the plant floor—examining products and looking for statistical variances from a standard. Many TQM initiatives were motivated by an external stimulus—a competitor, a customer, or a quality consultant—rather than an internally driven desire for continuous improvement. Once a TQM initiative is mandated by leadership, a natural response by workers is, "What do you think I'm producing now?" and homeostasis (staying motionless) digs in its heels.

My experience is that most workers want to produce the highest quality product or service possible. Few come to work wanting to produce mediocre output. Those who do are a product of a system that has repeatedly ignored worker involvement.

The Difference Between Planning and Implementing

My experience compelled me to ask, "What's the difference between planning and implementing the plan?"

I found that the planning process is well documented; in fact, volumes are written on planning. There is even a professional association for planners. I also found that most managers are well-versed in the planning process.

I remember a workshop on leadership I was facilitating. I was alluding to the differences between planning and implementation. The participants were all senior-level managers or business owners. I asked them to divide into small groups and quickly prepare an outline for a strategic plan. In less than ten minutes, we had a beautiful outline, one that any strategic planner would be proud to use. I then asked them to reconvene their small groups and tell me what they would do to implement the plan. After about twenty seconds of uncomfortable silence—then laughter—one participant finally stated her small group had an answer. It was, "Call a meeting, tell 'em what to do, and pray!"

The differences between planning and actually implementing the plan are profound. I realized that not understanding and valuing these differences was at the heart of my problem in trying to reconcile my education with real life experience. Developing a plan, whether for the initiation of flextime for the administrative staff or for a new corporate strategy, has several distinct characteristics:

1. *Planning is primarily a rational, logical, analytical process.* As I found in my early consulting, the first step in planning is to understand the forces at work that shape current reality. We somehow have to make rational sense (or at least understand the world within two standard deviations) of what is happening. This first step relies heavily on our rational, logical, and analytical skills.

2. *Planning is a mental exercise.* We have to summarize reality into something manageable so our minds can deal

with it. No small task, but thanks to computers and models and schema and Gannt and PERT charts and...well, you get the picture. We make mental representations of the world around us. We then manipulate our models (read: what if...), project our future, and, voilá, we get the basis for a plan. All told, a highly mental process.

3. *Planning, contrary to most current thinking, is typically event oriented.* Most companies have a planning period just prior to when the budget is due. Consequently, planning is episodic, or used when something goes wrong. As a result, planning is seen as an annual tool to use, not as a systematic part of a management style.

4. *Planning is "outside-in."* By this, I mean the planning process relies heavily on understanding the environment (the outside part) and developing a response to what is found (the inside part). This sequence is important to the planner. Why? Because plans are usually made in response to some external stimulus, situation, or event.

Implementing a plan requires a new mindset. In fact, instead of dealing with things, events, and data, we'll be dealing with people—people, like it or not, with the God-given right of independent free will. This means that implementation is, in many ways, the opposite of planning!

1. *Implementation deals with the behavior of people as opposed to the rational, logical, analytical process of planning.* And people are not always rational and logical. Our challenge is to have the behavior of the people who work with us be congruent with the direction of the organization—an awesome task.

2. *Unlike the mental exercise of planning, implementation deals with the emotions of people and their willingness to change.* Kurt Lewin, a professor at Harvard University, recognized this and developed one of the first theories of

change in the 1940s. His model, Force Field Analysis, says that to change the state of affairs in any situation, you must recognize that there are forces at work that support change (driving forces) and forces at work that resist change (restraining forces).

Take, for example, implementing a process re-engineering plan on the plant floor. The driving forces may be clearly identified in the "Process Re-engineering Report of the Plant Floor" that took nine months and untold thousands of consulting dollars to complete. Cost savings, quality improvement, and inventory reductions combine to make your product more price competitive and desirable in the market place. You can't wait for the next board meeting to announce record earnings and doubled market share.

But after two months of implementation meetings, you see that the reality is not quite so rosy. You say, "I feel like the captain of an aging, rusting ocean tanker. I order a change in direction...turn the wheel...there's a lot of clanging and clanking... everyone seems to be doing the right things...but nothing is happening. The damned thing just keeps moving straight ahead." What's going on here?

The restraining forces are winning, that's what. Let's take a look at the forces that typically resist change. You might find something like this:

"I'm not changing. Nobody asked me for my input." (*No involvement, no commitment.*)

"The way they're proposing to do things is stupid. Any moron knows it won't work." (*Can't see usefulness of change.*)

"I'm not going to do it that way; I've been trained to do it this way." (*Fear of either not knowing how to do new job or having to admit incompetence.*)

"Why do we have to change? What do they think we're producing now?" (*Assumption by management that, "Everything can be done better." True, until it's something "I" do. Then resistance sets in, and you say, "I'm not changing. Nobody asked me for my input."*)

I hope you're starting to realize that driving forces are typically logical, rational, pragmatic arguments. Restraining forces are usually emotional, behavioral, people-driven reasons to stay with the familiar and comfortable.

A common response when resistance to change occurs is to redouble our logical arguments for change. Train more (yell more?) and have more meetings. The result is usually more sophisticated resistance (read: sabotage) to the change. Until the emotional restraining forces are addressed, change will either not happen or occur at a high cost. Peter Senge, co-author of *The Fifth Discipline Fieldbook*, calls this "moving from compliance to commitment."[2]

3. *Implementation is an on-going process.* Unlike the event nature of planning, with a beginning, middle, and end, implementation is a minute-by-minute, real-time process. It's not something you do once—you can't have implementation day at the office. It's something you have to make a commitment to and do continuously, day in and day out.

4. *Implementation is "inside-out."* Implementation relies heavily on understanding human nature (the inside part) and being able to influence behavior to produce the result (the outside part) identified in the plan.

Herein lies the rub. This inside-out understanding is exactly what most of us were never taught in business school. And it's exactly this void that *RealTime Coaching* attempts to fill.

Planning and implementation are very different. But they're

not mutually exclusive. To be an effective leader, you need both skills: the ability to envision a future (planning) and the ability to mobilize people to implement what's necessary to realize that future (coaching). My experience, though, is that most successful managers are well-versed in planning… and most have a difficult time understanding why someone wouldn't buy into their logical arguments.

Implementation, then, requires significantly different skills from planning. Using outside-in skills ("You will do what I say") to implement is a sure prescription for disaster. *RealTime Coaching* is about implementation. It's what Warren Bennis, a professor and leading scholar on leadership at the University of Southern California, calls the "ability to translate vision into reality."

Dr. Ken Blanchard, noted management author, recently said:

> The role of managing has shifted dramatically in recent years. In the past, the emphasis was more on the manager as "boss." Today managers must be partners with their people; they can no longer lead from positional authority alone. Managers must move from a "command and control" role of judging and evaluating to a role of ensuring accountability through supporting, coaching, and cheerleading.[3]

What exactly does this mean? Let's look at an example.

The Coaching Dialogue

The following dialogue represents a *RealTime* coach in action. We'll look at a number of scenarios showing coaches and employees at work later in this book. In each one, you'll not only observe the interaction between coach and employee, but be privy to the coach's thoughts, as well. In this way, you get to learn what an effective coach says, and why he or she says it.

Now, though, just read the dialogue to get a sense of the way an effective coach can help an employee turn a negative and potentially nasty situation into a positive growth experience. Make notes or mark passages you think are especially important. We'll be revisiting this scenario in Chapter 8.

Fighting TQM

This coaching session takes place in the shipping department. Carol, the department head (Coach), is having a difficult time with Bill, one of her team members. Carol and Bill are good friends, but Bill is resisting the new Total Quality Management (TQM) program and bad-mouthing all the "measuring and meetings" the TQM program requires. It's a classic situation in which the planning has been great, but the implementation is leaving a lot to be desired.

Carol just received another CRS (Customer Rejected Shipment) from a long-time customer. In fact, several customer rejects can be traced directly to Bill's inattentiveness on the job. Due to the continuous manufacturing process, Bill's crew is the last to inspect the final product. Carol wants Bill to be more careful in releasing shipments to customers, a job he has done competently for more than ten years. Carol thinks the problem is in their manufacturing process, but Bill has been unwilling, up to now, to cooperate. Carol is going to try a different approach this time. With the CRS forms in hand, Carol goes out to the dock to talk with Bill.

Carol: Hey, Bill... got a minute? I need your help with something.

Bill: Sure. What's up?

Carol: Well, it's not exactly good news.

Bill: Oh, brother... another rejected shipment.

Carol: Yep. Another one. That's why I wanted to talk with you, Bill. I wanted to know if you had any ideas about what could be done to prevent this from happening in the future?

Bill: Uhh...oh, hey! I have a great idea! Why don't we call a meeting and start measuring something else?

Carol: No, no, I think we've had enough meetings around here. I'm serious, Bill. What do you think we need to

	do to keep from getting rejections like this one?
Bill:	C'mon, Carol. You know how it is around here. "Ship it today, ship it now, get it out the door." I'm under a lot of pressure here, and since we downsized, I've got five fewer guys on the crew. I'm trying to make up for all of 'em. And meanwhile, we've got this stupid TQM program going. All we do anymore is meet and measure, gab about quality and draw pictures. It's a waste of time, in my opinion. That's what I think.
Carol:	You know what I think, Bill? I think we have a problem shipping an unacceptable product, and, frankly it's jeopardizing a long-term customer relationship. I came out here to see if we could solve the problem, and I need to know whether or not you're interested in helping.
Bill:	Look, Carol, I'm not stupid. I can see it when the product coming off the line isn't up to snuff. But everything I'm hearing from the front office is "things are tight... work harder... get it out today... run the line faster." That puts me in a real bind.
Carol:	Yeah, I can see your dilemma. But if we could work out a way to get our quality back up where it should be, would that make your job easier?
Bill:	Sure. I mean, the people on the line know their work isn't what it should be. And you know as well as I do that the humidity in the plant and the temperature outside really mess with the performance of the equipment. I'd like to have a dollar for every time I told Harry or Alice the product was bad. It's getting to the point they hate to see me coming. I don't know what else I can do. So I just pass it through.
Carol:	Gosh, Bill, that doesn't sound like you—just passing through substandard work?
Bill:	I told you...I don't know what else I can do.

Carol: Well, that's exactly what I'd like to figure out. You've been here a long time, Bill. Is there anything you've been thinking about that could be done better if you just had more support?

Bill: I don't know. By the time the product gets to me, the horse is already out of the barn. At that point, the product is either acceptable, or it's not. I guess what I'm saying is, the people on the line need to know earlier in the run if something's wrong, so they can make adjustments.

Carol: So, if the operators knew earlier, they could make corrections. Is there anything you could do to make them aware of what's going on?

Bill: I'm not telling them anymore. Believe me, they've heard it enough from me. They just don't want to cooperate.

Carol: So, they're tuning you out. And their lack of cooperation is negatively affecting our customers?

Bill: Ha! You've got the rejects right there in your hand. You tell me.

Carol: And it goes even deeper than that. How do you think customer rejects affect our company performance and our profit sharing plan?

Bill: I'm sure they're not doing any of us any good.

Carol: No. And how is the lack of cooperation from the plant affecting you?

Bill: It's making my life miserable! So, why are you talking to me about it? They're the problem. Go talk to them.

Carol: I may do that, Bill. You've made some important points for improving quality. But for now, it sounds like this situation is affecting product quality, which is hurting our customers and our company. And you're miserable.

Bill: Well... I guess you can look at it that way.

Carol: So... what do you think we could do to improve com-
            munications?

Bill: I guess...I guess I could try to find another way to tell
            them they're producing substandard products. But I
            don't think they'll listen.

Carol: Look, let's say we did try once more and they didn't lis-
            ten. Would we be any worse off than we are now?

Bill: I guess not.

Carol: You know, you're right, Bill. We do need to work on
            better communication between you and the plant. How
            do you think we could do that?

Bill: Well...I hate to say this, but I think we need a meeting.
            Maybe you and me and Harry and Alice. Maybe that
            would be the best way to talk it out.

Carol: I think you're right. I'll arrange the meeting. In the
            meantime, could you jot down some items you'd like to
            cover? I'll put together an agenda...a very short agenda.
            I promise.

Bill: Sure. Thanks, Carol.

What did you notice about this conversation? Did you notice
Bill's hostility—his unwillingness to be accountable for problems
that were actually part of his responsibility? Did you see how he
put the blame for problems on the TQM program, on downsizing,
on the plant environment? Did you see him making excuses and
trying to justify poor quality product?

And what was Carol's response? Did you see how she refused to
accept Bill's rationalizations, how she wouldn't buy into his mock-
ery of the TQM program? Did you notice that she put responsibility
squarely on Bill while acknowledging that he had some valid con-
cerns? Did you see how she did this without finger-pointing—how
she actually got Bill to take responsibility for himself?

Perhaps most important, did you see how the conversation did-
n't end until there was a plan in place?

How is this conversation different from the one you would

have had with Bill in a similar situation? Chances are, there would have been more frustration and less resolution. That's because most managers have never really learned to be coaches. Fortunately, learning to be a great coach is what *RealTime Coaching* is all about.

We will revisit this dialogue in Chapter 8. After you have read more about the *RealTime Coaching* model you'll begin to understand why Carol said what she said and how she was effective in coaching Bill to help reduce the CRS's.

Chapter 1 Summary

Here are some of the important points I hope you've taken away from Chapter 1:

1. Change or continuous improvement is a necessary process in all successful businesses. Organizations that don't improve tend to wither and die.

2. All change comes with emotional costs: stress, fear, tension, and anxiety. In many cases, these very real challenges are ignored, to the detriment of the organization.

3. Planning deals with *things*, events, data, etc. It is:
   - Rational, logical, pragmatic
   - Mental
   - Episodic
   - Outside-in

4. Implementation deals with *people*. It is:
   - Behavioral
   - Emotional
   - Ongoing
   - Inside-out

5. A good manager is one who understands both planning and implementation. He or she knows that implementa-

tion is not an event, but a process that must be carried out every day in order for a plan to work.

6. *RealTime Coaching* is an effective method of helping managers implement their plans with their employees.

Now that you have a basis for understanding, it's time to give you some background. In Chapter 2, you'll learn the theory behind *RealTime Coaching*, how relationships between people drive results, and how the four principles of *RealTime Coaching* can produce change in your organization.

Footnotes

[1] Homeostasis is the ability or tendency of an organism or a cell to maintain internal equilibrium by adjusting its physiological process. *Homeo-* means same or similar, *-stasis* means a stable state. Thus, homeostasis is staying in the same or stable state, i.e., motionless.

[2] See Peter Senge et al. *The Fifth Discipline Fieldbook*, Currency, New York, 1994, Strategies for Building a Shared Vision, page 297.

[3] Ken Blanchard's Situational Leadership II, The Article, Blanchard Training and Development, Inc., 1994, page 3.

Chapter 2
Coaching: A New Way of Relating

You don't need anybody's permission to be a good leader, Lieutenant! All you have to do is be a resource to the team: know your people; look out after their welfare; keep them informed; let them take part in the decisions which affect them. Do this, and the team and you will succeed.

— Master Sergeant Emil W. Zacharia to Lieutenant Paul Giddens, U.S. Army, 1968

RealTime Coaching is based on solid, accepted behavioral theory that explains why we do what we do. But before we delve into exactly what *RealTime Coaching* is, let's spend a few minutes looking at the different ways people relate to each other in a working environment.

Three Different Ways of Relating: Do To, Do For, and Do With

You may not realize it, but there are three different ways all of us interact with other people. We can do things *to* people…we can do things *for* people…or we can do things *with* people. The results we get in our relationships are often a direct result of the form of relating we use.

"Do to" relating is common in parent-child relationships. "Pick up your room, or you can't go out tonight." "Finish your homework or you can't watch television." These are things I can do to a child because of my position of authority. I can enforce a negative consequence if the child doesn't behave in the way I expect. Of course, the consequences can also be positive: "I'll give you five dollars for every 'A' you get on your report card." "Finish your peas, and you can have chocolate cake for dessert." As a parent, this form of relating has a very important feature—it teaches a child that there is a consequence to his behavior. A problem arises when "do to" is the predominant way of relating between boss and employee.

Chances are, you know a few "do to" bosses, too. (Maybe you've even been one yourself?) The "do to" boss attempts to motivate with authority, and, again, the consequences can be both positive and negative: a raise or a promotion if the employee succeeds, loss of pay or position if the employee fails to live up to expectations.

What sort of relationship do you think most employees would have with a "do to" boss? Probably not a very good one. The relationship would probably be based, at least in part, on fear. Plus, the employees' motivation would be to avoid punishment—not to produce quality.

The carrot-or-stick school of management can become tiresome rather quickly, because there's always another judgment right around the corner. So even if you're succeeding, the "do to" boss is always on the lookout for an opportunity to be the enforcer.

Instead of relating at a "do to" level, you can choose to relate at a "do for" level. Again, this is a common way parents relate to children. In fact, when children are very young, parents necessarily spend a lot of time doing things for them. As children grow up, doing things for them can be a matter of convenience: "I don't have time to show you how to do that, so I'll do it myself." "Do for" relating can also actually grow out of a failure of "do to" relating: "I wanted you to cut the grass, but since you didn't do it, you'll have to go to your room, and I'll cut it myself."

The "do for" relating comes into play many times when attempting to delegate. Do I want to spend the time showing an employee how to do a task? Am I concerned about the quality of someone else completing the task? The answer often is, "I'll do it, it's just easier to do it myself."

I've seen plenty of "do for" bosses in my day. They're the types who are constantly taking over projects you thought were yours, making decisions they told you were yours to make and imposing their will on the project. They're the types who take on and keep too much work for themselves.

You can feel extremely frustrated working for a "do for" boss. The "do for" boss just won't let go, even though she may tell you she's going to. As a result, employees of "do for" bosses often feel resentful, as if they're spinning their wheels, going nowhere fast.

But what about the "do for" boss? What is she feeling? Resentment, frustration, probably. She's asking herself, "Why doesn't anyone take any initiative around here?" She never once pauses to think her "do for" style inhibits taking initiative. In fact, the boss is "training" her employees not to take initiative. Over time, the employee says, "Why try? The boss will do it for me anyway." So in reality, neither boss nor employee "wins" in this type of relationship. Is there an alternative? I believe there is. We call it "do with."

When you're doing something "with" someone else, you're partners. You can still be a guide or a mentor in a "do with" relationship. But you won't be a dictator. Ideally, parent-child relationships grow into "do with" relationships.

How about the "do with" boss? The "do with" boss says, "Let's look at this together and figure out our action plan." "Let's consider what's working and what's not working and see what we can do to make things better." Chances are, the "do with" boss will be one that employees like and respect—and enjoy working with. They feel part of a team and know their opinions and ideas will get a fair shake.

In short, becoming a "do with" manager is the first goal of the coach, because all good coaching relationships are "do with" relationships.

Bossing versus Coaching

Forming new ways of relating on the job may move you to examine your management style. Many of us use only one style of managing—one we learned from being managed ourselves.

In his book *The Control Theory Manager*, William Glasser spelled out some differences between what he called "boss management" and "lead management" (which we'll call "coaching"). The boss-manager:[1]

- Unilaterally determines tasks and sets performance standards, rarely compromises and insists that the worker adjust to the job as defined.

- Determines the consequences of substandard performance.

- Tells, rather than shows, how the work is to be done and rarely asks for worker input as to how the work might be done better.

- Inspects all work.

- Uses coercion to get compliance.

- Creates a workplace in which the workers and managers are adversaries and thinks this adversarial situation is the way it should be.

Sounds as if the boss-manager is the classic "do to" or "do for" boss. The coach, on the other hand, thinks differently, point for point. The coach:

- Engages the workers in an ongoing discussion of both the cost and the quality of work and listens and encourages workers to give input that will improve quality and lower costs.

- Shows or models the job so the workers can see exactly what is expected and thus increase their sense of control over their jobs.

- Eliminates most inspectors and inspections, and teaches workers to inspect or evaluate their own work for quality.

- Understands that the worker knows a great deal about what high-quality work is and how to produce it economically.

- Teaches that the essence of quality is constant improvement.

- Makes it clear that his/her main job is as coach and facilitator and provides workers with the best tools as well as a friendly, non-coercive, non-adversarial workplace.

Now, three questions:

1. How would you liked to be managed — bossed or coached?

2. How about the people you're managing — would they rather be bossed or coached?

3. And finally, what sort of manager do you think you are – a boss or a coach?

If you answered "boss" to the third question, that's okay. Most managers are bosses. But read on. You're going to learn an alternative approach.

The Three Basic Steps In Becoming A Coach

Theory is all well and good, and it can be eye opening to consider the differences among the three types of relating and the boss-versus-coach approaches to management. But what do you actually have to do to become a coach?

Figure 2

The Three Steps in Becoming an Effective Coach

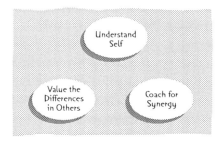

First, you have to *understand yourself.* Throughout this book—
and throughout your process in becoming a *RealTime Coach*—
you'll have many opportunities to gain valuable self-knowledge to
help you relate with the people you manage. You'll learn to recognize your strengths and your blind spots. And the self-discovery
evaluations you'll find in the chapters ahead will help you better
understand why you do what you do…so you can get a better handle on why others do what they do.

This is the second basic step in learning to become a *RealTime
Coach: valuing the differences in others.* "My way or the highway" is
boss-centered, "do to" and "do for" thinking. It's been said that
whenever two people decide to work together, differences will
arise. These differences can either lead to conflict—where both
dig in and try to "sell" the other—or synergy, where both respect
and value their differences as an opportunity to creatively solve
problems and develop mutually satisfying goals. As such, the
coach grows to understand that differences in people are not only
inevitable, but healthy. They can add strength and vitality to your
organization.

Third, as a *RealTime Coach,* you'll learn how to *adapt your own
behavioral style to create synergy* in your workplace. Just like all of
the people you manage, you'll learn that you have a preferred way
of behaving – a way you're most comfortable interacting with the
world around you. As a coach, you'll learn that your behavior isn't
a foregone conclusion. You can adapt it as different situations

arise, so you can deal most effectively with different people in your organization.

Keeping these things in mind – understanding yourself, valuing differences, and coaching for synergy – let's delve once again into the theory that underpins *RealTime Coaching*.

The Relationship Between People and Results

Unless we've gotten where we are today as the result of uncontrolled nepotism, all of us have our jobs for a sound reason. We are all employed by our companies in order to achieve a desired *result*; that is, our company expects to get a positive return – a better bottom line, a happier department, a higher profile, a more efficient operation – as a result of our employment.

How do you get results? Well, not by thinking about them. You can't think or feel your way to a result. Thinking and feeling are important behaviors and help us determine what to *do* next, but alone are insufficient to produce a result. In other words, achieving results means actually doing something. Results or performance, then, are driven by *behavior*. By this, I mean external, observable behavior: writing a report, returning a phone call, making a sales presentation, completing a task, etc. You hope what you do will achieve the desirable results you expect.

Why, then, do you do what you do? It's simple: we all behave the way we do because we want something. All behavior is driven by *wants*. And we all may want something a little bit different: a paycheck, a relationship, a job, a sense of accomplishment, a feeling of worth, a desire to make a contribution, or some combination of these and other wants. The fact is, we don't do anything unless there's some want behind it. So, even if you don't think you really want to do something ("I can't stand the thought of going to that party tonight."), your behavior will reveal some underlying want ("Harry will be there, and Rachel and Art, and I'll have a chance to talk with Ed about the Goldstone project.").

So then…if results come from behavior…and behavior is driven by wants…where do wants come from?

Figure 3

The Relationship Between Values, Wants, Behavior, and Results

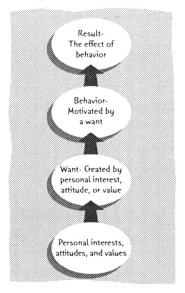

As we'll explore in greater depth in Chapter 3, your wants are manifestations of your *personal interests, attitudes and values*. We'll examine six basic values: the Theoretical, Utilitarian, Aesthetic, Social, Individualistic, and Traditional, and see how they affect your view of the world. For now, though, just understand that your values are linked to your wants, which are linked to your behavior, which is linked to the results you achieve. This chain forms the basis for the way a *RealTime Coach* works with employees to achieve positive results that make sense for both the employee and the organization.

The Four Principles of RealTime Coaching

Based on all of the above, let me introduce the four principles of *RealTime Coaching*. We'll examine each of these principles in depth and apply them in our goal of becoming effective coaches. But for now, just read them and see how they move up the values→want→behavior→result chain. In fact, these principles actually surround the chain (see Figure 4) and move logically from one point to the next and back to the start again. Here are the four principles:

1. What you want and how you judge the result you're getting is based on your personal interests, attitudes, and values.

2. The difference between what you want and what you perceive you're getting is the motivation for all behavior.

3. Your behavior is an attempt to close the gap between what you want and the result you perceive you're currently getting.

4. Achieving different results means either changing what you want or how you behave.

Figure 4

The Four Basic Principles of the RealTime Coaching Model

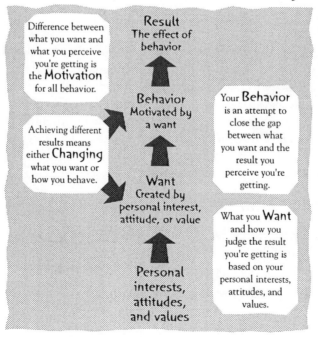

Difference between what you want and what you perceive you're getting is the **Motivation** for all behavior.

Result
The effect of behavior

Your **Behavior** is an attempt to close the gap between what you want and the result you perceive you're getting.

Behavior
Motivated by a want

Achieving different results means either **Changing** what you want or how you behave.

Want
Created by personal interest, attitude, or value

What you **Want** and how you judge the result you're getting is based on your personal interests, attitudes, and values.

Personal interests, attitudes, and values

As I've said, this is the theory, and understanding the theory is extremely important in making lasting, positive change. But it's the way we apply the theory in *RealTime Coaching* that truly makes the difference. These four principles lead to some logical questions that become natural parts of your coaching dialogue. Questions like:

- What do you want? Is what you want a direct reflection of your values? How does what you want relate to what the organization wants?

- What are you doing to get what you want? What actions have you taken? What exactly did you do? What are you doing now to get what you want?

- Is what you're doing helping you get what you want? Is it working? What's the gap between what you want and what you've achieved?

- If you're not getting what you want, what's your plan? What will you do next week? What do you think you need to do to get exactly what you want?

These are the key questions we use in *RealTime Coaching*. In one form or another, you'll find them throughout the dialogues, as our coaches try to help the people they manage match their personal goals with the goals and objectives of their jobs and their organizations. When this can be accomplished – when the employee and the organization both want the same thing, and the employee is behaving in a way to achieve the desired result – everybody wins and morale soars!

Chapter 2 Summary

Here are some of the important points I hope you take away from Chapter 2:

1. There are three basic ways of relating to people: do to, do for, and do with.

2. Coaching involves the development of "do with" relationships.

3. Employees will be more effective and productive when they are involved in "do with" coaching relationships than in boss-manager relationships.

4. The three basic steps in becoming a coach are: understand yourself, value the differences in others, and coach for synergy.

5. Results are a consequence of your behavior... behavior is a reflection of your wants...your wants are a manifestation of your personal interests, attitudes, and values.

6. The four principles of *RealTime Coaching* follow and surround this values→want→behavior→result chain, giving the coach effective tools to achieve the desired results.

7. In application, the four principles of *RealTime Coaching* lead to questions that become a natural and necessary part of the coaching dialogue.

That's the basic background. Now let's move to Chapter 3. You'll find a powerful tool you can use to help with your first task in becoming a coach – understanding yourself. You'll also learn more about the attitudes that shape our behavior, how different people are motivated by different values, and exactly what values are most important in motivating you.

Special Note—Please Read:

Chapter 3, "What's Your Passion?" and Chapter 5, "What Are You Doing?" discuss two powerful self-assessment profiles that we use in all of our *RealTime Coaching* workshops. The two profiles help you understand the values that motivate you (Personal Interests, Attitudes, and Values™ profile) and the behavioral style you use to get what you want (Managing for Success™ profile). Both profiles have been proven to be accurate across cultures and through decades of use. A sample copy of each profile appears in Appendix A and B.

If you would like your own personal 35-page profile that includes an analysis of both the values that motivate you and the behaviors you choose to get what you want in life, complete the order form in the back of this book or call Leadership Horizons directly at 1-888-COACH77 (US only, elsewhere 317-844-5587).

Footnotes

[1] William Glasser, *Control Theory Manager*, Harper's Business, New York, 1994.

Chapter 3
What's Your Passion?

Point of view is worth 80 IQ points.
> — Alan Kay, Director of Research
> Apple Computer Co.

In matters of conscience, the law of the
majority has no place.
> — Mohandas K. Gandhi

Since you've read this far, I assume you're motivated to find
out more about *RealTime Coaching*. Just why you're motivated is
something you'll probably discover for yourself as you continue
reading. This chapter and the three that follow, provide the basic
principles that are the theoretical basis for *RealTime Coaching*.

The four principles and coaching process are presented in a
sequential and logical format. In fact, many times a coaching session may progress more or less sequentially through the process as
presented. Other times the session may take unexpected side trips,
turns, and detours. This is to be expected. Human nature and the
coaching process are usually quite dynamic and fluid.

As you read the next four chapters, remember that the coaching process is not a recipe or rigid script to be followed, but a road
map of questions—each rooted in a principle—that forms the basis
for the conversation between coach and employee. The overall
goal is to develop a plan of action for change. When skillfully
used, the coaching process is a dialogue that helps the employee,
the organization, and the coach get exactly what each wants.

To help you remember the principles, we'll introduce an icon or symbol for each. In Chapters 8-11, we'll use the icons as "short-hand" in coaching examples to show how the theory is used in the coaching process.

Now, let's look at the first principle.

Figure 5

RealTime Coaching Principle 1

What you **want** and
how you **judge** the result you're getting
is based on your **personal interests,**
attitudes, and values

Discovering Your Passion

"What do you want?" It's an interesting question. The answer is a little bit different for everyone, even within the same organization. You might think, for example, that everyone in your company wants "to provide outstanding service that exceeds the expectations of our customers." You may have something like that written in a mission statement somewhere.

But reality is much different. "Outstanding customer service" may be a mission, but it's not really a desire. The question is, why do your employees want to provide outstanding customer service?

One employee may be motivated purely by financial considerations: "The better the service I provide, the more successful my company will be, and the better I'll be compensated." One may love pleasing people: "There's nothing I like better than seeing customers helped by a solution I've recommended." Yet another may simply like the challenge: "Great customer service is like a puzzle to me. I love figuring out the solution."

You might recognize these attitudes in a sort of vague way: Jim's a born leader, Trish is always helping others, Terry's analytical to a fault. Their attitudes are reflected in the way they behave.

But interests, attitudes, and values aren't readily observable. In

fact, sometimes they're difficult to discern at all. Therefore, you
can think of values as the hidden motivators of behavior—the
agendas that explain why people act the way they do.

Figure 6

Wants Are Reflections of What a Person Values

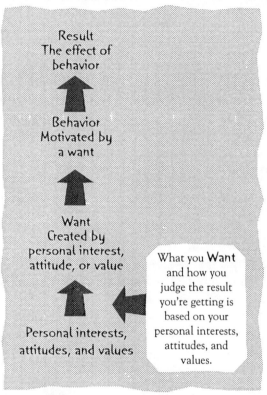

Result
The effect of
behavior

Behavior
Motivated by
a want

Want
Created by
personal interest,
attitude, or value

What you **Want**
and how you
judge the result
you're getting is
based on your
personal interests,
attitudes, and
values.

Personal interests,
attitudes, and values

Another reason the study of values is useful in coaching is that
it sheds light on how you interpret or filter what you're getting
back from life. Here's an example:

I remember leaving a movie theater recently with my wife,
Carol. The movie we had just seen was high on our viewing list.
We both had anticipated being entertained. But our experiences
of the movie were considerably different. I had thoroughly
enjoyed watching Harrison Ford take charge and win against all

odds as he played Jack Ryan in *Clear and Present Danger*. Carol, on
the other hand, was repulsed by the fact that governments could
be so cruel, heartless, and corrupt. Same exact movie, on the
screen at least, yet two totally different experiences. "What's
going on here?" I'm sure you've experienced this same kind of mismatch in your job: two people viewing exactly the same issue
experience it differently and act accordingly, at times to the
detriment of the organization's effectiveness, not to mention
their personal relationships.

The reason is, we perceive, evaluate, and judge events around
us through our values and interests. This particular principle is
extremely valuable when it comes to being an effective coach.
Each employee has a different spin on what the organization is
trying to accomplish and what he perceives he is getting from it.
As coaches, we have to realize that people rarely see the world in
exactly the same way.

The Six Interests, Attitudes, and Values

In *RealTime Coaching*, we recognize six basic values that motivate behavior. (I'm using "values" here to represent something we
value—something that holds our interest or is worthwhile to us.)
These values are identified as Theoretical, Utilitarian, Aesthetic,
Social, Individualistic, and Traditional.

These six values aren't something I made up. They were ini-
tially developed by Gordon Willard Allport, a Harvard-trained
psychologist, working with P.E. Vernon and G. Lindzey, in 1931.
Their "Study of Values," an assessment tool designed to help people understand the values that drive them, has been widely used
ever since, having gone through revisions in 1951 and 1961.

Allport's theories were further refined by Bill J. Bonnstetter, a
recognized expert in business education, who took findings from
the field of psychology and applied them to business. In so doing,
he developed new assessment tools that more accurately gauge
interests, attitudes, and values as they relate to the working environment.

Bonnstetter designed two instruments to measure two very different, but related, areas. One is a profile of behavioral style,

which we'll explore in Chapter 5. The other is the Personal Interests, Attitudes, and Values profile, that helps you see the sources for what you want. (See Appendix A and B for a sample of each profile.)

What's the purpose of these tools? First, by understanding your interests, attitudes, and values, you will be able to better understand what drives you every day—or in our *RealTime Coaching* model it's the values that drive what you want. Second, you'll be better able to recognize the underlying values that motivate others, even if they've never taken the Personal Interests, Attitudes, and Values profile. Third, you'll be able to relate values to behavior (again, more on this in a later chapter), adapt what you're doing to get the results you want and, through *RealTime Coaching*, help your employees do the same.

Discovering Your Personal Interests, Attitudes, and Values

As you read this section, see if you can determine your driving values–those values that are most important to you. While you may see yourself represented in many, if not all, of the values, you will probably have a strong affinity for one or two. These, then, would be your driving values. As an aid you may want to review the sample Personal Interests, Attitudes, and Values™ profile in Appendix A.

Here is a brief description of the six values.

A Passion for Knowledge: The Theoretical Value

A person with a Theoretical drive is primarily concerned with discovery of the truth—not necessarily spiritual truth—but literal, intellectual truth, knowledge for the sake of knowledge.

Theoretical people tend to take a cognitive attitude toward life. They look for identities and differences to help them make sense of the world. Theoretical people work by observation and reason, and tend to be non-judgmental about such intangible attributes as "beauty." Their interests are empirical, critical, and rational. As such, a Theoretical person may appear to others to be an intellectual.

Figure 7

Passions of the Theoretical Value

☐ Solving problems

☐ Objectivity in all areas of life

☐ Identifying, differentiating,
   generalizing, systematizing

☐ Intellectual process

☐ Discovery, understanding, ordering

☐ Pursuit of knowledge,
   identifying truth and untruth

☐ Knowledge for the sake of knowing

Now, how do these attributes affect the Theoretical person on the job? A Theoretical person will like to share knowledge, and like to be challenged intellectually, is good with data, and will usually be able to support his or her convictions. A Theoretical person is generally a good problem solver, and is good at integrating knowledge and experience to come up with solutions.

> *Coaching Tip:* When coaching someone with a high Theoretical drive, focus on the rational, analytical and objective nature of issues. Encourage him to use his cognitive abilities to draw conclusions and solve problems.

A Passion for Utility: The Utilitarian Value

Utilitarian people are interested in the value of time, resources, and money, and how they're used. Likewise, they abhor waste. Many times they are interested in the practical affairs of business: production, marketing, consumption of goods, credit, and the accumulation of wealth. They're motivated by security for themselves and their families. If you think of the stereotype of the average American business person—practical, conservative, status conscious—you have a pretty good picture of the Utilitarian person.

Figure 8

Passions of the Utilitarian Value

- Practicality in all areas of life
- Surpassing others in attainment of wealth
- Utilizing resources to accomplish results
- Gaining a measurable return on all investments
- Creative application of resources
- Producing goods, materials, services, and marketing them for economic gain
- Capitalism

Coaching Tip: From a coach's perspective, clearly, you can motivate Utilitarian people with money. While emphasizing financial aspects of a challenge may be off-putting to others, it's what really gets the Utilitarian's motor running. If you can focus on return on investment, you'll get the Utilitarian's attention.

A Passion for Beauty and Harmony: The Aesthetic Value

Aesthetic value indicates an interest in form and harmony. The Aesthetic person may judge each individual experience from the standpoint of grace, symmetry, or fitness, and life itself may be judged as a progression of events, each to be enjoyed for its own sake, even while it is appreciated in its totality. We should note that an Aesthetic person is not necessarily an artist, but does indicate a primary interest in the artistic episodes of life. This means that high Aesthetic people like to be recognized for their creativity.

Figure 9

Passions of the Aesthetic Value

- Practicality, appreciation and enjoyment of form, harmony and beauty
- Enjoyment of all senses
- Subjective experience
- Understanding feelings of self and others
- Self-realization, self-fulfillment and self-actualization
- Creative expression
- Appreciation of all impressions

They generally like to surround themselves with beauty and may have strong interests in nature, music, writing, film, or the visual arts. They may also be enthusiastic about sharing their enthusiasm with others. Aesthetic people are often good at seeing the big picture and developing creative solutions to problems. As such, strategic planning may be a strong suit for the Aesthetic.

Coaching Tip: As a coach, you'll want to focus more on subjective things with the Aesthetic than you would with the more objective Theoretical and Utilitarian people. Whereas the Theoretical person doesn't respond well to feelings, the Aesthetic person is very much at home here; in fact, she needs to relate to a challenge in this way. Focus on promoting harmony and personal fulfillment, plus removing discomfort, and you're well on your way to understanding how to motivate the Aesthetic.

A Passion for Helping Others: The Social Value

A Social person will have an inherent love of people and a desire to see others succeed. In its purest form, the Social value is selfless, indicating that the Social person can see people with other values as cold, heartless, or misguided. The Social person tends to place others before herself, and can be a kind and sympathetic listener.

Figure 10

Passions of the Social Value

☐ Investing self in others

☐ Selflessness

☐ Generosity of time, talents and resources

☐ Seeing and developing
the potential in others

☐ Championing worthy causes

☐ Improving society and
elimination of conflict

What does this mean in application? It means Social people can be selfless leaders and team players. It means they will value fairness in their negotiations with others. In business situations, they will be primarily concerned with value, giving customers the most for their money.

Social people will also tend to avoid confrontation if they think it will harm individual relationships they care about.

Coaching Tip: If you're coaching a high Social person, you'll want to focus on how his or her ideas will help others and maximize their coworkers' potential. As much as possible, avoid confrontation with a Social person: he's looking for harmony, not conflict.

A Passion for Power:
The Individualistic Value

An Individualistic person is interested in power. Note that many philosophers have seen power as perhaps the most universal and fundamental of all motives, since much of life involves struggle and competition. But an Individualistic person's wish for personal power and influence are uppermost.

Studies show that leaders in most fields value power highly. Which means that, in many cases, Individualistic people make good leaders. They want to be in control of situations. They want responsibility and accountability. They are not content to let others direct their work, but will seek to take the initiative to guide their own destiny.

Figure 11

Passions of the Individualistic Value

- Leading others

- Achieving position

- Advancing position

- Forming strategic alliances

- Attaining and using power to accomplish; purpose

- Planning and carrying out a winning strategy

- Tactics and positioning

> *Coaching Tip:* Coaching an Individualistic person can pose some interesting challenges. You'll definitely want to help the high Individualistic person understand how a given situation can increase her power or advance her position within the organization. You might also want to focus on the effect of that power: how the Individualistic person's position strengthens the organization as a whole.

A Passion for Meaning:
The Traditional Value

People characterized by the Traditional value are interested in unity and order. They like rules and structure, and will usually seek out a code, often a religious system, for living. In many cases, Traditional people will be conservative politically and socially. They will judge others based on their own belief systems.

Figure 12

Passions of the Traditional Value

☐ Understanding the totality of life

☐ Finding meaning in life

☐ Pursuit of the divine in life

☐ Following and dying for a cause

☐ Living consistently according to a "closed" book

☐ Converting others to their belief system

> *Coaching Tip:* In practice, this means that
> Traditional people are excellent at following tradi-
> tional guidelines. It also means they need to have
> a light at the end of the tunnel, that they'll follow
> the rules when they can see that doing so leads to
> a higher purpose. If you can get a Traditional per-
> son focused on an ideal you want him to reach,
> you'll have success in motivating him.

Six core values—Theoretical, Utilitarian, Aesthetic, Social,
Individualistic, and Traditional. All very different, and all present
in differing degrees in each one of us. The key is finding which
are the values you hold most dear, and which are least important
to you. Doing so will help you understand what you want, what
others want, and how to work together more effectively.

"But I Still Don't Like Broccoli!"

So, if everyone has the same six core values, what makes us
different? The differences lie in two areas. The first is, people have
differing *intensities* of these six core values. The second is, people
make different *choices* about how to satisfy their values.

You may want to stop here and think about the intensities of
your interests. Think back over your life: your career choices, your
childhood family, your current family, where you live, your social
life and the friends you have, the organizations in which you're
active. How do the life choices you've made reflect the intensity
of your values?

Now think about all of this in relation to the two driving values you identified earlier. Do you see a connection? Can you
detect patterns in your life that correspond to the highest scores
in your profile? Do you see needs that are going unsatisfied and
creating tension in your life? For example, if you have a high
Aesthetic value and you're working in a small office with no windows, no pictures on the walls, and no music, you might be feeling

stressed. If you have a high Individualistic value and there seems to be a bottleneck above you in the corporate pyramid, it may be affecting your attitude toward your day-to-day work.

The second key to understanding the role of values in your life is knowing how they influence the choices you make about satisfying your wants. The point is, the intensities of your wants and the way you go about satisfying them form the basis for who you are and the motivation for your behavior.

While it is difficult to generalize about wants, some common examples I've experienced include:

- *Utilitarian and Individualistic:* Seen in many entrepreneurs. They want to make choices, are willing to live with the consequences, and seem to enjoy the risk that freedom and independence offers.

- *Social and Traditional:* Characteristic of religious leaders. Helping others within a religious framework is stimulating to them.

- *Theoretical and Utilitarian:* Noticed in professional service careers, such as consultants and accountants. Mission is to "Make money from knowledge."

- *Aesthetic and Utilitarian:* Blends beauty and money. Seen in leaders of architectural firms, landscaping companies, and home decor retailers.

- *Social and Individualistic:* Combines a desire to lead with a desire to help others. Seen for example, in leaders of not-for-profit social service agencies.

Regardless of the mix and intensity of their values, everyone has some desire to be recognized for his or her contributions to the organization, to feel worthwhile. As you might expect, you feel most worthwhile when your passion values are being satisfied. For example, let's say you have a high Traditional value. You know that your work is valued by the company; after all, you've kept your job for a number of years. But you never see your work leading to anything. You're never truly aware of your company's big picture. So your primary passion value is not really being satisfied through your job, leading to restlessness and anxiety.

In my experience, this need for feeling worthwhile—regardless of a person's values—is often overlooked. But it is a significant way to increase employee productivity and executive effectiveness. Simply telling an employee that her contribution is really helping the company as a whole to achieve its goals goes a long way toward keeping her job satisfying. A simple recognition, authentically given, is a powerful need-satisfying gesture.

The take-home message here is that every employee has basic values that are important, and that each has a unique way of satisfying his or her needs. This icon—a gift—will be used throughout the text to represent something of value to us. When you see it, remember to focus on the wants of an individual–what a person wants is a representation of what they value.

Figure 13

A "gift" icon represents what a person wants

What Do You Want?

An important role of the coach is to explore needs and wants with the employee and attempt to match them with the goals and objectives of the organization. Discovering what the employee wants—from her job, her co-workers, you, and others— is a required step in the coaching process. (In the next chapter, we'll use the information about what employees want in order to understand motivation).

Just asking, "What do you want?" may seem simple. In reality, it is an extremely difficult question for many employees to answer, for a number of reasons:

- First, some employees have *never* had the experience of their employer asking them what they want. Their experience is so ingrained—punch in, the boss tells you what to do, you do it, the boss evaluates your work, and you punch out—that the mere hint they may have a say in their work elicits suspicion.

- Second, many may see their job as a paycheck, not something to be enjoyed. Asking, "What do you want?" begs the obvious reply: "A paycheck. Why do you ask?"

- Third, they may know exactly what they want, but answer "I don't know," anyway. This answer protects them from potential embarrassment ("You want WHAT?") or disappointment ("Sure, that's great, but we can't change company policy just for you."). It also may be motivated by fear of what you might do with the information. ("His wants are simply incompatible with our goals as a company.")

Getting a clear indication of employee wants is a challenging, and integral, step in the coaching process. It's tough to get an honest answer, and some employees may resent the perceived invasion of their privacy. As a coach, you're asking the employee to share his inner world of wants[1] with you. To do this, he must become vulnerable, which requires trust.

The degree to which an employee chooses to become vulnerable is directly related to the level of trust in the relationship. What the employee is weighing in his mind is: "Can I trust you? Can I be honest and will my wants be taken seriously? Or will they be used against me later?"

The More/Start/Stop/Continue Process

Let's take a closer look at the "What do you want?" question. We're trying to identify what the employee finds valuable in his job, what is useful to him, what is perceived as helping him satisfy his interests, and adds value to him, his job, and the organization.

In situations where I want clients to start thinking more critically about their jobs, I've found a very simple, yet powerful, way to start a dialogue on wants. I call it the "More, Start, Stop, Continue" process. It goes like this:

"I'd like you to think about your job, all the things you've done over the past months, and identify those activities that:

- You would like to do *more* of.

- You're not now involved in or doing but would like to *start* doing.

- You get little enjoyment from and you'd like to eliminate from your job, or *stop* doing.

- You enjoy and would like to *continue* doing.

Sometimes, you can reap big rewards with simple tools. The resulting dialogue is usually rich with wants, interests, desires, and preferences.

The "want" question also has an implied future aspect to it. By this, I mean that a currently satisfied want is not going to be mentioned. An employee will typically mention only what she wants but does not have now. Questions on how things could be better, such as: "Is there anything you're doing you could do better if you just had more time/support/resources?" can lead to valuable discussions about what the employee wants and deems valuable.

Lastly, "want" questions can be helpful in continuous improvement. In discussing past unsatisfactory situations, rather than finding fault or blaming, useful questions are: "How would you like it to have turned out?" "What part do you think was done well?" "What part do you think could be improved?" or, "If we had to do it again, what would you change or do differently?" The ensuing dialogue can be an avenue for identifying quality improvement ideas in an atmosphere of openness, trust, and honesty. Here are some examples of questions that explore what a person wants.

Figure 14

What do you want? How to identify needs and wants.

Tell me what you want.
What do you want from me?
If you had a magic wand,
What do you want?   what would you change?
Do you really need that
or do you just want it?
If you had what you want
what would you really have?
Are you getting a sufficient
amount of satisfaction from your job?
What do you think your boss, subordinates,
other team members want from you?

Do you have enough fun on the job?
Is this what you want or is
What do you want to see?...
it someone else's goal?
hear?... experience?

What do you think your   What would you   What would you like
team wants from you?   like to have happened?   to accomplish?

Do you want more
freedom in your job?
What do you want to change?

If you could design a perfect hour; day;   Who do you admire? Why?
week; month; year; what would it include?
What do you want less of in your job
What do you want to have?   that you're getting too much of now?

What are you trying to achieve?   What do you really want?

What do you want on your job   What do you want to be saying?
that you're not getting now?
Tell me what your ideal job would include.

What is your goal?   What's important to you?   What is your expectation?

What do you want to be   What do you want more of in your job
thinking? doing? feeling?   that you're not getting enough of now?

Chapter 3 Summary

Here are some of the things I hope you've learned in Chapter 3:

1. The first principle of *RealTime Coaching* is: What you
   want and how you judge the result you're getting is
   based on your personal interests, attitudes, and values.

2. Psychologists have identified six basic values in all people. They are the Theoretical, Utilitarian, Aesthetic,
   Social, Individualistic, and Traditional.

3. All of these values are present to varying degrees in each of us. The values we hold most dear form the basis for our personalities and are the hidden factors that motivate our behavior.

4. Not only do we have the same needs in varying degrees, we also go about trying to satisfy these needs in different ways. The ways we try to satisfy our needs can be defined as our wants.

5. One of the coach's most critical roles is to identify employee wants, see how they relate to the employee's core values, and try to find ways to match these wants with the goals of the organization.

6. The More/Start/Stop/Continue process can be an effective tool for helping the coach explore wants with employees.

Now that we've considered values and wants, and you've gotten some insight into your own personal "hidden motivators," it's time to take a closer look at motivation in general: Why people do what they do. On to Chapter 4 and *RealTime Coaching* Principle 2!

Footnotes

[1] William Glasser (in *The Control Theory Manager*, Harper Business, New York, 1994), identifies our inner world of wants as our "quality world." This quality world stores, in memory, high need-satisfying experiences. Our behavior then is our attempt to control the real world so that it is as close as we can make it to our quality world.

Chapter 4
Why You Do What You Do

Real freedom is the ability to pause between stimulus
and response and in that pause choose.
— Rollo May

Reengineering doesn't change what needs to be changed
most: the way people at all levels relate to the enterprise.
— Margaret Wheatley
Leadership and the New Science

In Chapter 3, we saw that what people want is tied directly to
their unique personal interests, attitudes, and values. So how
come people can't always get what they want? Because what you
want is only one arm of the scale. The other arm is what you perceive you're getting. The real question becomes: Is your scale in
balance or not; that is, how does what you want match up with
what you think you're getting? This leads directly to our next
RealTime Coaching principle:

Figure 15

RealTime Coaching Principle 2

The **difference** between what you **want**
and the **result** you perceive you are getting
is the motivation for all behavior.

It is believed that we as human beings have literally billions of synapses in our brain, all used for comparing.[1] In practical terms, we are constantly comparing what we want with what we perceive we're getting at the time. These comparisons create the energy that motivates all human behavior.

This is the energy that causes members of any organization to show up for work on Monday. While everyone's reason is a little bit different from everyone else's—for some it's a paycheck, for others, a chance to use their skills and talents, and still others, a social time for meeting and enjoying others' company—the underlying motivation is an urge to close the gap between what they want and what they perceive they are currently getting.

Figure 16

Motivation is internal and is caused by a mismatch between what people want and what they perceive they are getting

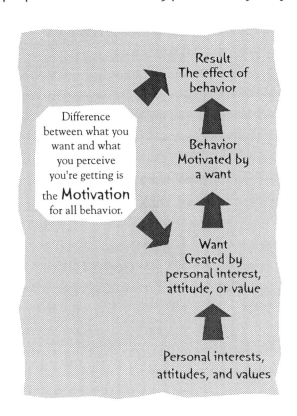

Difference between what you want and what you perceive you're getting is the **Motivation** for all behavior.

Result
The effect of behavior

Behavior
Motivated by
a want

Want
Created by
personal interest,
attitude, or value

Personal interests,
attitudes, and values

This move to a state of equilibrium, where needs are satisfied, is a common phenomenon. Like homeostasis mentioned earlier, an object at rest will remain at rest. Plants grow toward sunlight. Steam turns to water in the absence of heat. Birds fly south to maintain their comfortable climate. And, in statistics, it's called the theory of central tendency (the bell shaped curve).

Motivation is From Within

A subtle yet extremely important part of this second principle is that motivation is generated *within an individual*. Since the motivation for behavior is the result of a *mismatch* (between what a person wants and what he perceives he's getting) *and* both wants and perceptions are under the control of the individual, motivation for behavior is generated entirely within the individual.

This is a powerful principle and can begin to change the way we look at behavior. For example, consider the following:

- Bill is an outgoing, friendly fellow who was recently laid off from his job in the audio visual department of a large insurance company. To make ends meet, he took a night position as a front desk clerk at a nearby suburban motel. After three weeks, he quit. *What motivated Bill to quit?*

- Teresa is a very creative graphic artist. For the past eight years, she has worked as a freelancer for several advertising agencies. During a recent business "dry spell," she was offered and accepted a job at one of the agencies. After four months of great work, for no apparent reason, she became irritable, short-tempered with her colleagues, sullen, and withdrawn. Her work suffered, and she was asked to leave the agency. *What motivated Teresa's change in behavior?*

- Steve is an ambitious, bright, and energetic marketing representative for a large manufacturing company, who is being considered for a promotion. The new position requires extensive travel to several different cities. Steve and his wife just had their first child. Steve recently asked his boss not to consider him for the promotion.

Why did Steve want his name removed from consideration?

Each of these examples can be better understood by applying the principle of motivation. First, each person wanted something from his or her job. Bill was used to more social interaction and was by nature very outgoing. Teresa, after eight years on her own, liked the freedom and independence of being a freelancer. And Steve wanted a job that did not require being away from his family. All found themselves in the untenable position of not getting what they wanted, even when their jobs seemed to have some real advantages. *Their behaviors, then, were their best attempts at the time to meet their needs.* Bill quit his job, Teresa got herself fired, and Steve removed himself from the promotion list.

The behavior we observe in others can be seen as their best attempts to get their wants met at the time. We may disagree with their behaviors, we may object to their methods, we may not understand their motives, but we must realize that these behaviors are their best attempts to get what they want. As we'll fully develop later, your role as a coach will be to encourage employees to examine and evaluate their behaviors and help them identify and use new behaviors that will better get them what they want.

Here, then, is the second of the icons we'll use as reminders of *RealTime Coaching* principles at work. We'll use a *scale* icon to represent a comparison. On one arm of the scale is what we want. On the other arm is what we perceive we're getting. The scale being "out-of-balance" reminds us of a mismatch.

Figure 17

**A scale represents self-evaluation that compares
what we want with what we perceive we are getting**

So Who Can Motivate the Employee?

Does this principle of motivation shed any new light on the age-old question: "Can a manager motivate a worker?" Our answer is, yes and no. Motivation, as we've said, is the energy created within a person when she is aware that what she perceives she's getting does not match what she really wants. The greater the mismatch, the higher the motivation.

Since we can't control what goes on inside someone else's mind, a coach *cannot* directly motivate an employee. But an effective coach can *influence* what an employee wants, how she goes about getting what she wants, and how she perceives what she's getting. So, in a sense, yes, an effective coach can motivate another worker, albeit indirectly.

I remember a vivid example of this when I was trying to motivate my twelve-year-old stepson, Blake, to do his arithmetic homework. We'd been around and around on the usefulness of learning long division. But Blake couldn't see any usefulness at all. The homework held little value to him and his internal motivation for long division was zero.

We took a well-deserved break from homework and happened to catch the player introductions for a Chicago Blackhawks' hockey game on ESPN. Hockey is Blake's favorite sport, the Blackhawks his favorite team, and goalie his favorite position. As the Blackhawks' goalie was introduced, the announcer said he had an impressive "save" percentage of 94.8%. Blake quickly told me that that was extremely good. Seeing my chance, I asked him, "How do they calculate a save percentage?" He was stumped, and I knew I had him.

A quick look at his *Hockey Yearbook* told us that a save percentage was calculated by taking the number of shots against the goalie that didn't result in a goal, divided by the total number of shots on goal. I got the morning newspaper and told Blake that last night the Hawks won 2-1 and there were 28 shots on goal. I then asked Blake, "What was the goalie's save percentage last night?" After some "coaching," he divided 27 by 28 and told me, "He had a great night! He had a 'save' percentage of 96.4%!"

This little example demonstrates the power of internal motivation. Blake was not at all interested in doing long division just for the sake of doing long division. No amount of persuading could change that. The best I could hope for was compliance, "do your homework or else," not commitment. But when he couldn't calculate a save percentage (and he *wanted* to know how), his scales became out of balance and his motivation to learn long division increased. As Blake's coach, I influenced what he wanted. As a result, he learned long division—what I wanted!

Self-Evaluation:
The Cornerstone of Effective Coaching

As is clear in the above example, effective coaching is dependent on the ability of the coach to get the employee to *self-evaluate* and *self-disclose* what he wants and what he's getting. If there is a mismatch, energy is created that is the source of motivation. What the coach wants the employee to do is answer this question: "Are you now getting what you want?" In the example above, Blake's motivation came from wanting to know how to calculate a save percentage. Learning long division was a way to satisfy that want.

It is crucial to effective coaching that the *employee* self-evaluate or self-judge his performance—not the coach. While this may seem to be a subtle point, it is in stark contrast with the traditional management philosophy of boss-centered evaluations, reviews, and critiques.

One reason for the coach to withhold judgment on an employee's performance is that the judgments are futile attempts at stimulus-response management. Judgments are akin to saying, "This is unacceptable, you must change." It typically doesn't work and is resented by the employee.

Another reason for withholding judgment is the consequence of a boss-invoked evaluation of performance. My experience is that there will likely be one of two outcomes from boss-centered judgments:

- If the evaluation is positive, the employee will likely cease to improve above the boss's standard, be satisfied with current performance, and not foster continuous improvement.

- If the evaluation is negative, regardless of how helpful it is or how compassionately given, the employee's attention will be more focused on evaluating the evaluator—in this case, the boss—than on improving his own performance.

The process of self-evaluation, I hope you see, is directly related to this principle. The coach is trying to discover—for the employee, the coach, and the organization—what the employee's motivation is for his or her behavior. In order to do this, the coach's questions encourage the employees to make value judgments about what they want, what they perceive they're getting, and the direction and speed their behavior is taking them. Sometimes all that is needed is a gentle prod, by the coach, to encourage self-evaluation. The sudden awareness created by the evaluation can help refocus energy and redirect behavior.

The coach's questions do not seek to directly identify the wants, perceptions, or behaviors (that's done later), but simply to have the employee evaluate and critically examine his wants (and underlying values), perceptions, and the behavioral choices he's making to satisfy his wants.

As you may imagine, the variety of questions a coach might ask an employee to help that employee evaluate wants is limitless. The focus, though, is in three broad areas:

1. First, is a critical comparison of the mismatch between "wants" and "perceptions" of reality, such as, *Is what you're doing getting you what you want?* As an example, a coach might ask, "Did your preparation pay off?" or "Did you get what you wanted from Paul?" or "Did you get the reaction from the audience that you expected?"

2. An evaluation of the direction and speed the behavior is taking the employee toward what she wants, such as,

*"Is what you're doing moving you in the right direction?...
Are you moving fast enough?"* Here, a coach might ask,
"Are you pleased with your progress in the training program?" or "Did your conversation with Linda help
improve your relationship?" or "Do you think we'll
make the deadline?" or "How does your performance
compare with where you want to be?"

3. An assessment of the usefulness and attainability of the
   goal (or "want") and the perceptual filters used to evaluate results, such as, *"Is your goal realistic?... Does it add
   value?"* and *"Is it helpful for you to look at it that way?"*
   Questions a coach might ask are, "How do you think
   Bill's promotion will affect morale?" or "What in your
   mind would be a 'win'?" or "How does your plan fit with
   what the other team members want?"

As an example, consider this brief dialogue and note the
coach's emphasis on encouraging Pat to evaluate his wants, direction, and perceptions. (The comments in italics are the thoughts
and intentions of the coach and are not part of the spoken dialogue.)

Coach: Hey, Pat, how's the new sales program going? *(Self-eval-
          uate the direction and speed of the new program.)*

Pat: Not well at all. Sales aren't nearly what we expected.
          (Mismatch.)

Coach: So, you're not getting what you want? *(Checks out mis-
          match.)*

Pat: Nope. *(Confirmed.)*

Coach: What do you think you need to change? *(Evaluate how
          you're looking at the problem.)*

Pat: Maybe the attitude of the sales force. Other than that,
          I don't know. *(Excuses.)*

Coach: They're not supporting you, huh? Do you have some
          ideas on what to do next? *(Evaluate how you're looking
          at the solution.)*

In this brief dialogue, we can see how Pat is viewing the situation and his perception of the problem. We can also see how the coach's questions guided Pat's evaluation process. Here are some questions that will encourage self-evaluation:

Figure 18

**Is what you perceive you're getting what you really want?
How to encourage self-evaluation.**

Is what you're doing moving you in the right direction?... Are you moving fast enough?

How's it going?

Are you getting what you want?

Are you satisfied with the results?

Does it help you to look at things that way?

Can you get there from here?

What looks good to you?

Is it better or worse?

Is it helping?

Can you get what you want with these changes? This plan? Your current level of commitment?

What do you think is in your best interest?

Is what you want realistic and attainable?

Is what you're doing getting what you want?

Do you like it the way it is?

How would you evaluate your progress?

On a scale of 1-10, how well do you think you're doing?

What did you achieve?

How will this add value to your performance?

What do you think you need to change?

How do you feel about the result?

Is what you're doing against any rules, policies, or procedures?

Is continuing to do that going to get you what you want?

On a scale of 1-10, how would you evaluate your key relationships on the job?

How committed are you to making these changes?

Is what you're doing helping or hurting you?

Is that what you want?

If you could do it over, what would you do differently?

Is what you're doing (or plan to do) worth the consequences that might result?

Chapter 4 Summary

Here are the key points to take away from Chapter 4:

1. The second principle of *RealTime Coaching* is: The dif-

ference between what you want and the result you perceive you are getting is the motivation for all behavior.

2. As human beings, we're constantly—although not
   always consciously—making this comparison between
   what we want and what we think we're getting.

3. Self-evaluation encourages employees to critically evaluate how they are trying to satisfy their wants, the
   direction their behavior is taking them, and the usefulness of their wants.

4. While a coach might not be able to directly motivate
   an employee, the coach can encourage and foster the
   self-evaluation process and match the employee's goals
   with those of the organization.

So we've considered our wants and the six basic values that
influence them. We've shown that the mismatch between our
wants and our perceptions is what generates our motivation.
What does motivation lead to? Behavior, of course. That involves
the third principle of *RealTime Coaching*, which is the subject of
Chapter 5.

Footnote

[1] William Glasser, *Control Theory*, Harper & Row, New
York, 1984, page 163.

Chapter 5

What Are You Doing?

95% of American managers today say the right thing.
Five percent actually do it.
                    —Fortune, February, 1994

Try? There is no try. There is only do or not do.
                    —Yoda,
                          in The Empire Strikes Back

In our last chapter, we saw that our behavior is motivated by an imbalance between what we want and what we perceive we're getting. Essentially, then, our behavior can be defined as our best attempt to get or maintain balance in our internal scales. This is the cornerstone of our next *RealTime Coaching* principle:

Figure 19

RealTime Coaching Principle 3

Your **behavior** is an attempt to
close the gap between what you want
and the result you perceive you're getting.

In our *RealTime Coaching* model, this principle links what people want with the results they are achieving.

Figure 20

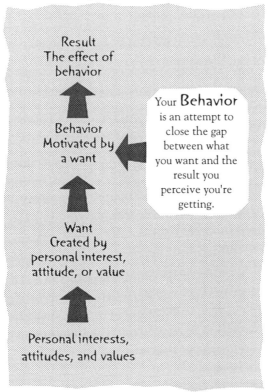

Why a person behaves

Result
The effect of
behavior

Behavior
Motivated by
a want

Your **Behavior**
is an attempt to
close the gap
between what
you want and the
result you
perceive you're
getting.

Want
Created by
personal interest,
attitude, or value

Personal interests,
attitudes, and values

Behavioral Style and Management Style

Let's consider an example to help shed light on this important principle. Say that sales have been down for the third quarter in a row at Allied Sales Company, and management has asked its four regional sales managers to report on what they think is causing the problem and what can be done about it.

First, all four sales managers are hard workers. They all need their jobs, and they all want the company to succeed. The mismatch – scale out of balance – is the difference between what they want (sales growth and job security) and what they perceive they're getting (poor sales and job insecurity).

Susan is the Northeastern sales manager. Her first response is to get angry. Sales are down only slightly in her territory – in spite of poor economic conditions and trouble with delivery from the home office. The folks in the other territories must be really letting the company down. Nevertheless, Susan swings into action quickly. She doesn't wait for analysis: she hands down tough new policies on sales calls and personally monitors salesperson productivity every week. She takes charge. In the process, she alienates a few of her salespeople, but they probably didn't have the drive she was looking for anyway.

Gary is the Midwestern sales manager. His first instinct is to call a meeting. He assembles salespeople from across his territory to discuss the issues and try to develop solutions. He takes this challenge very personally, but is enthusiastic and positive about turning the trend around. He makes an inspiring opening talk to his salespeople, imploring them to get on board and work hard, to look for ways they can improve and share them with the group. Gary won't tolerate negativity – every idea is a good idea, even to the point that some of his salespeople begin to wonder if he is really focused on coming up with a solid plan.

Alex is the Southern sales manager. Not one to wear his heart on his sleeve, Alex is nonetheless deeply troubled by the slow sales and is determined to come up with solutions. He is intensely loyal to his salespeople and wants to see each one of them succeed. In fact, one source of his frustration is he knows that several of his salespeople are underperforming, and he just can't bring himself to let them go. Alex doubles his own workload and develops an extensive plan for turnaround, which he e-mails to every salesperson. He starts working sixteen hours a day and is committed to personally doing whatever it takes, for as long as it takes, to ensure his team's success.

Wendy is the Western sales manager. At first, Wendy is puzzled. She has always been a stickler for policy, and has always made certain her team did everything by the book. So if sales are down, she's certain there must be something wrong at the corporate level. For a week, she is deeply critical of corporate policies, even while feeling great anxiety over the potential loss of her job. Finally, though, she begins to rationally assess the situation. Some policies are out of whack, and she finds documentation to show how some changes could be made to cut costs and increase salesperson efficiency. After carefully considering all the data, she implements several changes in her territory and carefully monitors the results.

One problem. One goal. Four decidedly different behavioral responses. One takes charge and issues orders; one forms committees and searches for answers; one works harder and tries to put the team on his back; one digs for facts and analyzes trends. What's going on here?

What's Your Behavioral Style?

As we've seen, people can pursue the same goal for very different reasons. But values are really not at issue here. The issue is behavior. So ask yourself: "Which style best describes how you might have responded to management's request?"

Just as we have identified six different basic values we all share to varying degrees, so have we identified four core behavior types. We have another profile (see Appendix B) that will help you determine which core behavioral type you are—after which we will look at the four basic behavioral styles in more detail. After the evaluation you may want to order your own personal profile. Instructions on ordering are given at the back of the book.

Take a few minutes now and read through the word groupings that follow[1]:

Group 1	Group 2
Ambitious	Expressive
Forceful	Enthusiastic
Decisive	Friendly
Direct •	Demonstrative
Independent	Talkative
Challenging	Stimulating

Group 3	Group 4
Methodical	Analytical
Systematic	Contemplative
Reliable	Conservative
Steady	Exacting
Relaxed	Careful
Modest	Deliberate

Which group of words *best* describes you *most* of the time? If you are having a difficult time making a choice (and many of you will!), have three or four close friends, trusted co-workers, or a spouse identify the group they think *best* describes you. You will usually hear a consensus, so listen closely to what they say.

If you chose:	Your behavioral style is probably a:
Group 1	Core "D"
Group 2	Core "I"
Group 3	Core "S"
Group 4	Core "C"

The D, the I, the S and the C represent four different dimensions of your behavior—or how you go about achieving results on the job. The **D** stands for **Dominance** and indicates your approach to tasks, problems, and challenges. The **I** stands for **Influence** and describes how you attempt to influence people. The **S** stands for **Steadiness** and tells how you respond to the pace or speed of the environment. The **C** stands for **Compliance** and indicates how you respond to the rules, regulations, policies, and procedures set by others.

Style Characteristics

Now that you've determined your own core behavioral style, think back to the example we used at the start of this chapter. If you had been placed in a similar situation, how would you have responded? Do you feel an affinity for one of the sales managers?

The aggressiveness of Susan? The enthusiasm of Gary? The methodical approach of Alex? Or the analytical approach of Wendy? Does his or her response match up with your core behavioral style?

The fact is, we all have different styles of behavior we use to get our scales in balance. While we have a preferred, or core, style, our behavior on the job (and elsewhere, for that matter) is a mix of all four behavioral dimensions. What makes each individual unique is how he or she mixes and blends each behavioral dimension. Chances are you'll be coaching a variety of people representing all four behavioral styles, so let's take a closer look at each of the four core styles.

The Core D—The Decisive, Direct, Task-Oriented Person

The first behavioral dimension deals with how we respond to tasks and challenges. This is the D, or Dominance, dimension. Here are the outstanding characteristics of the Core D person.

Core D's have an inherent need to direct. They crave authority and responsibility. Generally, they are extroverts and leaders, forceful and determined people. Core D people love challenges, and will quickly tire of repetitive activities. In relationships they will readily confront conflict. They're always looking for the next mountain to climb.

Core D's, it will probably not surprise you to learn, love to win. They want to win in everything: business, golf, the weekly football pool, everything. Other behavioral types like to win too, but for different reasons. For the Core D, challenge is the reason, the desire to be on top, to prove it can be done. They can also be risk takers. They don't see failure as an option. They charge ahead, oblivious to whatever, or whomever, gets in their way. They're not trying to hurt anyone, they just have their eyes on the prize.

Of course, Core D's have limitations, too. They can overstep authority. They can be bossy, impatient, and argumentative. In relationships their directness may be too confrontive at times. They tend to not listen well. They can overload themselves with tasks, take on too much. They can push people rather than lead them effectively. And they can be too task-oriented, not caring enough about the people involved.

Here's a summary of the readily observed behavior of Core D persons—their unique characteristics and some of their blindspots.

Figure 21

Unique Characteristics and Potential Blindspots of the Core D (Dominant) Behavioral Style

Unique Characteristics	Potential Blindspots
Results oriented	Act or speak before thinking
Fast paced, ability to make decisions quickly	Impatient
Desire to win	Create fear in others
Willingness to state an unpopular view	Too high risk
Risk taker	"Juggle" too much at once
Argumentative, quick to challenge	Interrupt and not listen well
	Quick to anger

What would be an ideal working environment for a Core D? One in which she has the ability to control her own destiny, where she's evaluated on results, not methods, where the work is always challenging, never routine, and she has plenty of opportunity to express her ideas. Anything else is a compromise to the Core D.

In communicating, Core D's are direct, to the point. They may come across as blunt or impolite. Here are some tips on how to coach the Core D effectively:

- Be clear, specific, and to the point. Stick to business. Don't ramble or make small talk; a Core D will become impatient.

- Come prepared. The Core D wants things in a well-organized package of logically presented facts. Remember: don't waste their time.

- Ask specific questions, not rhetorical ones. Core D's prefer "what" questions.

- If you disagree with a Core D, take issue with the facts, not the personality. Try not to be offended by the way a Core D argues; instead, focus on the content of the argument.

- Provide an opportunity for a win/win situation. Don't force the Core D into a losing position. They hate losing.

This information can be extremely important in your attempts to coach Core D people. Whenever you suspect you're dealing with a Core D, review this material to help make your coaching as effective as possible.

Core I–The Expressive, Enthusiastic, People-Oriented Person

Now let's move on to the next core style, the Core I. The I stands for Influencing, and Core I people seek to influence others with personality, warmth, and emotions.

What about Core I characteristics? First, the Core I needs to interact with others. They like to verbalize. They'll talk at length, and tend to use friendly contact and verbal persuasion to inspire you to their point of view. The Core I needs to be liked. They sometimes like everyone, and have a great need for social acceptance.

The Core I is incredibly optimistic. They'll tend to see the good in every situation. And they are involved in lots of situations. They are also highly involved people. They can promote trust and confidence, and believe they can persuade people to behave in a desired fashion.

The Core I is often a very emotional person. They don't have very good poker faces. They wear their hearts on their sleeves and because of their inherent optimism, this expressiveness can be contagious. The Core I can inspire others to jump on the band-wagon because they believe so strongly.

What about limitations? The Core I has a tendency to over-sell, over instruct, and over delegate, to not know when to be quiet. They can act impulsively, without thinking. They trust people indiscriminately, even people who shouldn't be trusted. In relationships they will flee from conflict when possible, fearing the conflict will damage the relationship. The Core I can be inattentive to detail and have difficulty planning and controlling their time. They tend to overestimate their ability to persuade others. They may be good listeners, but only situationally. They may be too expressive and emotional during times that call for more restraint. Again, look at these limitations as areas where they can improve.

Here's a summary of the readily observed behavior of a Core I—their unique characteristics and some of their blindspots.

Figure 22

Unique Characteristics and Potential Blindspots of the Core I (Influencing) Behavioral Style

Unique Characteristics	Potential Blindspots
Creative problem solver	Talk before thinking
Enthusiastic, natural optimism	Lose track of time, often late and hurried
Humorous	Abandon position in conflict
Fun loving	Disorganized
High contactability, trusting of others	Overly trusting
Ability to make others feel welcome or included	Overly optimistic, can be superficial

What type of job takes advantage of the Core I? One with lots of people contact. They can be good at motivating groups and setting up contact networks. You want to give them freedom of movement, without the need to handle a lot of detail. Ideally, a Core I should have a democratic supervisor, not a dictator.

Here are some tips on how to coach the Core I effectively:

- Interact with them in a way that supports their ambitions. Don't legislate or muffle.

- As opposed to the Core D, do make time to socialize with the Core I. Core I like small talk and want personal relationships.

- Talk about people and their goals with the Core I, not just facts and figures. They want to know about the personal consequences of any action.

- Ask for their opinion. Listen. Be patient, not so task oriented.

- Provide the Core I with ideas for implementing action. Don't waste time dreaming or brainstorming, they might see every idea as a good one.

- Provide a fun, stimulating forum for them. Don't make meetings too short or businesslike.

- Finally, offer the Core I immediate incentives for taking risks. Don't take too much time, or they'll take all the time you have—usually talking. Get to the action items.

Core S-The Methodical, Reliable and Team-Oriented Person

Next comes the Core S. The S stands for Steadiness or how a person responds to the pace or speed of their work environment.

Here are the basic characteristics of the Core S, beginning with the need to serve. The Core S loves to help out, wants to lend a hand to get the job done. Serving energizes them.

Core S's tend to be intensely loyal. They don't change jobs often. They'll stay in relationships for a long time for reasons of harmony. This means Core S's can be very adaptable to varying situations. They're good at modifying their behavior to achieve the harmony they crave.

Core S's are patient and relaxed and can be viewed as deliberate, laid back, and unemotional. They're cool and rarely rattled—at least on the outside. Although they can be very active emotionally, Core S's don't show their emotions readily. They hide their problems. As leaders, they have been known to take their teams to great heights even while enduring incredible personal struggles.

Core S's want long-term relationships. They are highly attached to their teams, their companies, their friends, and their families. They operate well within their groups, and will strive to maintain the status quo.

Closure is essential to the Core S. You have to allow a Core S to finish what she starts. Leaving a job undone is an incredibly stressful situation to them. As you might expect, Core S's don't like to have too many balls in the air at the same time. They like completeness. They don't want to watch a movie if they can't see the end, or didn't catch the start.

Naturally, Core S's also have some limitations. They may take criticism of their work as a personal affront. They will resist change for change sake. They may need help getting started on new assignments, can have difficulty establishing priorities, and will wait for orders before acting.

Core S's tend to internalize feelings that should be let out in the open. In relationships they will tolerate conflict and will be slow to confront problematic relationships. They tend to be too hard on themselves. They may also cling to a project long after it should have been given up. And the fact that they don't project a sense of urgency can be frustrating to others.

Here's a summary of the readily observed behavior of a Core S—their unique characteristics and some of their blindspots.

Figure 23

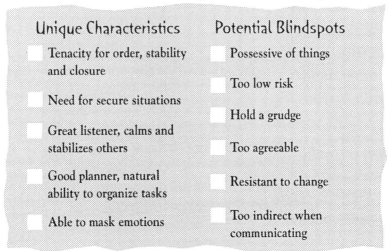

Unique Characteristics and Potential Blindspots of the Core S (Steady) Behavioral Style

Unique Characteristics

Tenacity for order, stability and closure

Need for secure situations

Great listener, calms and stabilizes others

Good planner, natural ability to organize tasks

Able to mask emotions

Potential Blindspots

Possessive of things

Too low risk

Hold a grudge

Too agreeable

Resistant to change

Too indirect when communicating

In terms of managing a Core S, you would give her jobs for which there are existing standards and methods, and put her in an environment where she can develop long-term relationships. The Core S wants to deal with people personally and intimately. You want to give the Core S personal attention for a job well done. A great environment for a Core S is one that is stable and predictable, and allows time for change.

In communicating with the Core S, you'll want to start with a bit of small talk. Break the ice. Don't rush into business. Similarly, show your interest in the Core S as a person. Find out what the Core S likes and dislikes. Here are some tips on how to coach the Core S effectively:

- Don't force quick responses from the Core S. Give them time to develop their opinions, then be a good listener.

- Present your case logically and non-threateningly to them. Don't make a show of power or be demanding.

Realize the Core S's feelings may be hurt if a situation impacts them personally.

- Core S's like "how" questions. They willing respond to being included in the decision-making process.

- Be casual, informal, not abrupt, rapid, or too businesslike.

- Don't mistake the Core S's willingness to go along as satisfaction.

- Give them personal assurances and guarantees, and never promise what you can't deliver. Remember, the Core S wants trust.

Core C – The Analytical, Exacting, Quality Conscious Person

Now we come to the final core type—the Core C—which stands for Compliance or how a person responds to the rules and regulations set by others.

Here are the Core C characteristics, beginning with the need for procedures. Core C's go by the book. They're very aware of and sensitive to the dangers of mistakes and errors, and take a disciplined approach to problem solving. As you might expect, a lot of quality assurance people are Core C's. Core C's have a tendency to be driven by fear—fear of making a mistake or doing the wrong thing. In this regard, Core C employees are the most quality conscious. They're low-risk people, preferring to go by the book.

Core C's, more than anything, want a stable and orderly life. If you give them a way of doing things that works, they'll stick with it. Core C's are perfectionists. They compete with themselves, constantly striving to do things better. They always want to do things the right way, meaning they'll usually come down on the safe side of the problem. Core C's are risk-averse people.

Core C's are precise and attentive to detail. They're great gatherers of data and facts and careful in everything they do. They crave proof. "In God we trust, all others use data," is a great description of the Core C. Don't make statements to Core C's unless you can back them up.

Core C's, like the other styles, have limitations. Here are a few. Core C's are hesitant to act without precedent. They tend to overanalyze and get bogged down in details. They're prone to analytical paralysis. They can be too critical of others and defensive when challenged. In relationships they will avoid conflict when possible. Core C's don't always make great salespeople. They tend to *tell* ideas rather than *sell* ideas. And, as you might expect, Core C's are generally too hard on themselves.

Here's a summary of the readily observed behavior of a Core C—their unique characteristics and some of their blindspots.

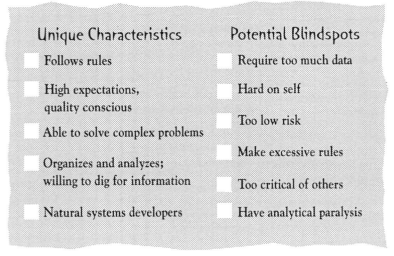

Figure 24: **Unique Characteristics and Potential Blindspots of the Core C (Compliant) Behavioral Style**

Unique Characteristics	Potential Blindspots
Follows rules	Require too much data
High expectations, quality conscious	Hard on self
Able to solve complex problems	Too low risk
Organizes and analyzes; willing to dig for information	Make excessive rules
	Too critical of others
Natural systems developers	Have analytical paralysis

So what kind of environment is ideal for the Core C? One where critical thinking is demanded and rewarded. One where assignments can be followed to completion. Technical, task-oriented work, with a minimum of noise and people, is great for the Core C. And it should be an environment in which quality and standards are important.

It should be no surprise to you that the best way to communicate with the Core C is to plan your case in advance. Don't be disorganized with the Core C. Here are some tips on how to coach the Core C effectively:

- The Core C likes things straightforward and direct. Don't be too casual and informal.

- Be thoughtful. Consider all sides of an issue. Don't force them into quick decisions.

- Present the Core C with specifics. Remember, they like data and information. And don't be vague about your expectations.

- Although you should draw up an action plan in all coaching situations, it's especially important with the Core C. Core C's like dates and milestones.

- If you disagree with them, make sure you have the facts to back you up. Opinions and feelings won't cut it with the Core C.

- Give Core C's time to make decisions. Be careful of trying to "close" with the Core C. She needs time to weigh the facts and make her decision. Also, be careful about physical closeness with the Core C, she prefers a little space.

Now let's briefly review the four behavioral types by taking another look at the words that describe them.

- **D:** Ambitious, forceful, decisive, direct, independent, and challenging.

- **I:** Expressive, enthusiastic, friendly, demonstrative, talkative, and stimulating.

- **S:** Methodical, systematic, reliable, steady, relaxed, and modest.

- **C:** Analytical, contemplative, conservative, exacting, careful, and deliberative.

Remember: all of these dimensions are present in every one of us and represent our "total behavior." Each is a continuum, not a black or white choice. By learning to appreciate and work with all types of people, we help everyone grow and prosper. (See Appendix B for a sample behavioral profile.)

We Choose Our Behaviors

Here are the insights we can learn from Principle 3. First, "total behavior" is an intertwined bundle of all four behavioral dimensions. While we all have strong preferences in one behavioral dimension, many behaviors are available to us—we choose them—in our attempts to regain control, get what we want, balance our scales, or simply accomplish a task. This means all four behaviors act in concert as our way of responding to an out-of-balance situation.

Secondly, we always have control of the *doing* component of our behavior. And if we significantly change what we're doing, we will also change the result we're achieving or the outcome of our actions.

This is one of the most powerful lessons of this third principle. While we all have different interests, attitudes, and values that motivate our behavior, we choose our behavior. We may have a preferred style of behavior, but what we actually do is nonetheless a choice.

This seems a simple enough concept. But in reality, it can be extremely difficult to put into practice. There have probably been many times in your life that you've felt frustrated: "I've tried everything and nothing works." Actually, you've probably tried the same thing over and over again. Remember, you have a preferred behavioral style that you think is going to help you close the gap between what you want and what you perceive you're getting.

The power of *RealTime Coaching* is helping others understand when what they're doing isn't getting them what they want, then prompting them to make changes in their behavior *or* in what they want. *RealTime Coaching* focuses not on the underlying values that motivate people, but on what they want and and what they're actually doing.

In fact, we can think of our observable behavior as "playing our role." We'll use a *director's clapboard* as our icon to represent our "action."

Figure 25

A director's clapboard represents a person's action

Behavior. Wants. And results.

In coaching, we see "behavior"—what a person is doing—as the link between what he wants and the result he's currently achieving.

The employee's awareness of his behavior is crucial to his understanding of his effectiveness in fulfilling his wants and the goals of the organization. Also, by being aware of his chosen behaviors and making a self-evaluative judgment as to the effectiveness of the choice, the employee can then move toward self-directed improvement.

Here's what a competent coach should know about behaviors:

- First, feelings (or emotions) are powerful indicators of whether or not wants are being met. Negative emotions are a sure sign that scales are out of balance—that there is a difference between what we *want* and what we perceive we *have* at the moment. The bigger the disparity, the more the scales are out of balance, and the more intense the emotion. If you find yourself in an emotionally charged situation, be aware that scales are out of balance and that wants are not being satisfied. (In a later coaching session, we'll demonstrate ways to deal with highly emotional situations.)

- Second, my experience as a coach with many executives reveals that people are *most* aware of what they are thinking and feeling and *least* aware of what they are doing. This observation is supported by Choice Theory. Coaching, then, will necessarily focus on increasing the employee's awareness of the doing component of our coaching model or how they're going about getting what they desire.

- Third, while we may be least aware of our "doing" behavior, it is the most easily changed. We'll see in the planning part of coaching (the future behavior, covered in Chapter 6) that we focus exclusively on what an employee is going to do to better meet his needs and the objectives of the organization.

These three points are the foundation for increasing an employee's self-awareness of the behavior she is using in each dimension of her behavioral style. The coach will ask the employee to identify precisely, "What are you doing?" to get what she wants. If the employee's behavior is balancing her scales and providing value to the organization, you usually have a highly motivated employee. If not, the coach can help the employee develop new behaviors that are more in line with her wants and the goals of the organization.

What You're Likely to Hear When You Ask, "What Are You Doing?"

You'll typically hear a lot of generalities when you ask an employee to recall a particular event or situation and describe the behaviors he used. Keep in mind that the employee is least aware of his "doing" behaviors.

As an example, if you asked Pat, your sales manager, "What did you do at the sales meeting?" his response might be, "I tried to get the sales force fired up about the new promotional plan." What you're hearing is his intention of what he wanted to accomplish, *not* what he did. If you then asked one of the sales associates, "What did you do at the sales meeting?" you might hear, "I got real excited about the new promotional plan." What you're hearing is a feeling, *not* what they did.

This type of communication is quite acceptable for social small talk, but let's change the situation: It's two months hence, and the promotional program is a miserable failure. You're the vice president of sales and marketing and you want to review what was done at the sales meeting. By asking specific questions about the "doing" behavior of the sales manager, a much different picture might emerge on the effectiveness of the sales meeting. (The italicized words are not part of the spoken dialogue.)

Coach: Hi, Pat. Say... how's the new sales promotion plan doing? (*Evaluation.*)

Pat: Lousy. Our promotion plan isn't generating orders, and sales are considerably under our projections. (*Mismatch.*)

Coach: Pat, review for me what has been done so far. Maybe we can see something in hindsight that we could do differently. Do you have a copy of the agenda from the sales meeting two months ago where we introduced the new plan? (*What did you do?*)

Pat: Well... I don't think I prepared an agenda. (*What wasn't done.*)

Coach: How about the samples? Were they distributed like we talked? (*What have you done?*)

Pat: No. The supplier was late, so I thought I'd give them out next month when we get together. (*Excuses.*)

Coach: How about the product information packets? Were they sent out last month to our customers? (*What have you done?*)

Pat: No, shipping was bogged down and they didn't go out until last week...Hmm, I think my hindsight is becoming pretty clear. (*Self-evaluation.*)

It may take some time for you to develop the skill of reviewing behavior in a non-judgmental way, but the reward in terms of self-evaluation by the employee can be immense.

In Chapters 8–11 when you see *RealTime Coaching* in action, we'll provide you tips on how to adapt your style for effective coaching.

For now though, here are some suggestions on questions you can use to increase awareness of behavior:

Figure 26

What are you doing?
How to increase self awareness of total behavior.

What are you doing?

What have you done so far?

Describe your mood when...

What are you doing when you feel most productive?

What did you say? What was the tone of your voice?

What did you do? Think? Feel when that happened?

What actions have you taken?

What are you thinking?

What did you tell yourself when...?

What do you think your body is telling you?

What were you doing... thinking... the last time you felt really good?

What are you doing now?

What were you doing the last time you felt important?

If I were there what would I see? Hear? Feel?

How do you spend most of your time?

Describe how other people act who are achieving their goals.

What were you thinking the last time time you felt important?

What are you feeling?

How would you describe what you did?

What were you doing... thinking... the last time you felt a sense of belonging?

What were you doing... thinking... the last time you felt a sense of achievement?

Describe how other people you admire act.

Chapter 5 Summary

Here are the most important things to remember from Chapter 5:

1. The third principle of *RealTime Coaching* is: Your behavior is an attempt to close the gap between what you want and the result you perceive you're getting.

2. Just as we respond to the six basic values to different degrees, we also have "styles" to our behavior – certain ways we are most comfortable trying to get our needs met.

3. The four core behavioral styles in the DISC model used in *RealTime Coaching* are: Dominant, Influencing, Steady, and Compliant. Each of us prefers one of these behavioral styles.

4. Recognizing an employee's core behavioral style is critical in helping him overcome challenges on the job, get his scales in balance, and fulfill the needs of the organization.

5. Behavior is chosen. If what we're doing isn't working to get our scales in balance, we can always choose different behavior.

6. Although we choose our behavior, it is often the most invisible aspect of our personalities to us personally. The coach's job is to help employees recognize when what they're doing isn't working and develop a plan to do something different.

Develop a plan...sounds like another *RealTime Coaching* Principle. On to Chapter 6!

Footnotes

[1] This process to determine a person's behavioral style and
the subsequent discussion on style characteristics is from
The Universal Language DISC: A Reference Manual
(Target Training International, Ltd., 1993) by Bill J.
Bonnstetter, Judy I. Suiter, and Randy Widrick.

Chapter 6
You Gotta Have a Plan

There are usually two reasons why companies fail to ade-quately plan. When things are going awfully bad—they don't have time to plan—they're too busy fighting fires. And when things are going quite well—they're too busy enjoying their success—they don't want to rock the boat!

To have his path made clear for him is the aspiration of every human being in our beclouded and tempestuous existence.

— Joseph Conrad

I have always thought that one man of tolerable abilities may work great changes, and accomplish great affairs among mankind, if he first forms a good plan, and makes the execution of that plan his sole study and business.

— Benjamin Franklin

Up to this point, we've done a lot of talking and studying. We've had some insights into our hidden motivators. We've seen why we do what we do, and how we go about doing it. Now it's time to apply what we've learned:

Figure 27

RealTime Coaching Principle 4

Achieving different results means **changing** either what you want or how you behave.

An objective of the coaching process is to match the employee's wants and behavior with the goals and objectives of the organization. This is achieved by applying this fourth principle to effect change. The previous three principles—evaluating and building awareness and stressing responsibility—are important and necessary parts of coaching, but they alone are insufficient in improving performance. In essence, what we are doing in this plan is specifically identifying a set of *future* behaviors we believe will improve the effectiveness of the individual to meet the goals and objectives of the organization.

Figure 28

A Plan Identifies Future Behavior

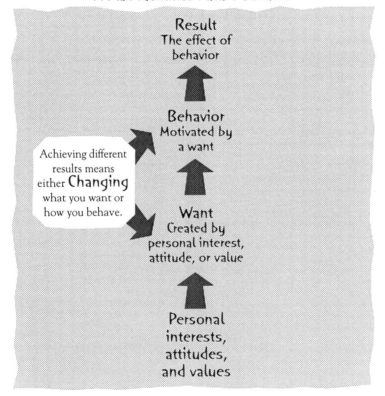

My experience is that this last step, while not difficult, is the Achilles heel of the coaching process. Plans are often vaguely defined, don't focus on the doing or acting behaviors, or are overlooked altogether. This oversight can significantly reduce the value of coaching. Again, the whole reason for *RealTime Coaching* is to provide you with the tools to create a more productive and satisfying workplace.

To remedy this situation, a competent coach uses a plan to signal closure of the session. A good plan:

- *Is collaboratively developed with the employee and the coach.* Since coaching is a "do with" process that seeks to satisfy the needs of the employee and the coach and achieve the goals and objectives of the organization (assuming the coach is representative of the corporation), collaboration is essential.

- *Is simple—nothing complex or complicated.* Keeping the plan simple and straightforward increases the likelihood of commitment, accomplishment, and satisfaction.

- *Usually identifies only two or three objectives as the next steps.* The emphasis is on being able to accomplish something quickly. This keeps the process fluid and avoids the formality of a larger planning process.

- *Is time dependent.* A specific schedule is determined for the completion of the plan.

- *Focuses on the doing component of total behavior.* As stated before, this is the part of total behavior over which we have most control. It is also the only behavior that can effect change in the organization.

- *Is measurable.* The accomplishment of the plan is not up for debate. Either something occurred or it didn't. Therefore, it's measurable.

This part of the coaching process is so important, it merits its own icon. The clipboard will represent the necessity of developing a plan for change in each coaching session.

Figure 29

A clipboard represents a plan for change

Now, here's a simple coaching dialogue that demonstrates closure with plan development:

Coach: Where do you think we ought to go from here, Pat? (*Collaboration on some next steps.*)

Pat: I need some time to research our sales trends and talk with shipping on those information packets. And I'd like to see if we can get those samples any sooner. But first I want to check with our regional managers to get their thoughts and I'll summarize them in a memo to you. Then I...... (*Too much!*)

Coach: Whoa! That's a pretty full plate. What do you think is the one thing that would be most useful for you to do right now? (*Keep it simple.*)

Pat: Hmm... My head is spinning with ideas right now. I think I need some time to collect my thoughts and write them down. Then I'd like some help on prioritizing them. Could we meet tomorrow morning and I'll show you what I have? (*Good, focuses on doing and collaborating, with schedule and measurement.*)

Coach: Well, that's three things! But I like where you're headed. Let's meet first thing at 8:30 and we can prioritize your list. (*Specific.*)

Pat: Great! See you then.

A useful plan is critical to being a good coach. To give you some additional guidance on the questions used for planning, see the examples that follow.

Figure 30

What's your plan?
How to develop a plan for change.

What will you do in the future?

What will you commit to doing?

What do you need to do to get what you want?

Is there anything else you could do?

What are you going to be saying to yourself?

What's your deadline for achieving this goal?

Tell me how you're going to do that.

What do you need to start doing to change your direction?

What's your plan? Your next steps?

What would help you become a more effective employee?

On a scale of 1–10, what's the likelihood of your plan succeeding?

What evidence would there be to show you attained your goal?

What do you think you need to do next?

What do you think would happen if you did that?

How are you going to go about it?

When will you start?

What should you do the next time that happens?

What do you want to do?

How are you going to talk to that person?

What's your plan to increase your satisfaction on the job?

Which course of action do you prefer?

What do you think you need to do now to move toward your goal?

How would you know if you reached your goal?

What do you think you need to do right now?

Chapter 6 Summary

Our behavior, expressed through how we approach tasks, how we influence people, how we respond to the pace of the work day, and how we respond to the rules and policies set by others, is how we get what we want. We choose certain behaviors as a way to balance our scales. In other words, we strive to match what we want with our perception of reality through the behaviors we choose.

Planning in *RealTime Coaching* focuses on the doing or behavior component of the *RealTime Coaching* model and is a crucial part of the coaching process. What will be done in the future to better get our wants and the organization's goals met is our objective.

Now that we have all the theory, it's time to get an in-depth look at how to put *RealTime Coaching* into practice.

Chapter 7
Put Me In Coach, Put Me In!

coach (kōch): 1. One who gives private instruction, a private tutor. 2. Coach was used to mean a "tutor" or a "trainer" in allusion to the speed of stagecoaches and railway coaches. (In the days before automobiles and airplanes, the fastest method of travel was by coach.) 3. A coach, then, is an instructor, who brings his students along at the fastest possible rate.

> — Derived from kocsi, after
> Kocs, Hungary, where such
> carriages were first made.

With apologies to Julia (Childs) and James (Beard), they can only teach you how to make their soufflé. If you want to create your own, you must first try to understand why eggs and flour rise—or don't rise—when you do certain things to them, and then begin to develop your own theories, which result in the dishes you create.

> — Bill Backer, Former Vice Chairman
> and Chief Creative Officer
> Backer Spielvogel Bates Worldwide Inc.
> The Care and Feeding of Ideas

RealTime Coaching: Making It Happen

You now have a powerful arsenal of tools to help you begin coaching. A review of each principle and related icon follows. The icons are used as a form of shorthand to show how the principles influence the coach's thoughts and actions.

But before we start coaching, I want to explain how you can begin becoming an effective coach. I've divided my comments into two sections.

First, I'll cover the coaching relationship. I want you to think about the perceptions or filters you have about people—about managing and leading—and encourage you to begin evaluating if your current perceptions will help or hinder your progress in developing your coaching abilities.

Second, to help get you started quickly, I'll give you a "starter kit" of coaching techniques: tips I've found particularly useful. I'll help you relate these skills to the four principles to help you bridge theory and application.

"What You're Doing is Speaking So Loudly I Can't Hear What You're Saying!"

Have you ever been in a conversation where you were hearing the right words but your "gut" told you something different? Maybe it was at a social gathering, or with a new customer, or possibly a candidate you were interviewing for potential employment. You liked what you heard, but that little voice said, "Be careful, watch out, don't decide right now."

Your attitudes and underlying perceptions about managing people in general and the person you're coaching are communicated when you coach. *What you're communicating about yourself is as much in the words you choose and the questions you ask as it is in the way you do it.* Simply put, ask yourself, "What do I want this person's 'little voice' to be saying about me right now?"

My experience tells me that to be an effective coach:

> *The coach wants the team to win. Do you want the employee to succeed?* You have to want the employee to succeed and constantly strive to match his or her wants with the goals and objectives of the organization. The skills demonstrated in the cases that follow can be manipulative if based on anything other than a desire to support and collaborate with the employee, not blame or find fault. The employee, or the people you manage, must

believe that you want to resolve any problem in an atmosphere of trust and mutual satisfaction. In essence, do you want the employee to succeed?

It's no use walking anywhere to preach unless your walking is your preaching, said St. Francis of Assisi. The same goes here. If you, the coach, are not getting your needs met, if you bad-mouth your superiors, if you don't self-evaluate your work, then don't expect your employees or the people you manage to conform to a higher standard. Remember, coaching is about forging a "do with" relationship–not a "do to" or "do for." Some practical pointers include: Asking your employees if they feel supported by you. Do they feel you are working *with* them? Do they have the resources necessary to do their jobs? And, do they feel like you are a resource that makes their job easier?

Give up your old, ineffective management habits of control, coercion, command, or manipulation to gain cooperation. One of the most difficult habits to break is your desire to maintain control or power over another. With practice and experience in *RealTime Coaching*, you will come to realize that your desire for personal power and control inhibits quality, and is, in fact, an illusion anyway. This shift, though, will not be easy for you. There is a long history in American business that supports stimulus-response management practices: the boss is the stimulus and the employee is the response. The hierarchical nature of most organizations even perpetuates this belief. Resolve to cease using these ineffective skills and learn *RealTime Coaching* skills.

You really have to listen. Your effectiveness as a coach is directly related to your ability to empathetically listen. You must sincerely want to learn what the employee wants, and see the value in better matching his wants with the goals and objectives of the organization. Your ability to listen, without judgment, builds the necessary trust so vital to being an effective coach. A management truism is: "Show them how much you care by listening and then they'll care how much you know."

You need to set realistic boundaries. RealTime Coaching is not a panacea, nor does it provide an excuse for accepting incompetence on the job. All organizations have certain guidelines and policies that govern how they function. Organizations today have to produce quality products and services. This can be achieved only when effort and energy are focused on need-fulfilling work, continuous improvement, and producing the highest-quality products and services at the lowest possible cost.

You have to stay in the here and now. One of the most demanding skills of *RealTime Coaching* is staying in the present. Letting your mind wander or not listening intently will surely compromise the quality of the coaching session. Being able to stay focused—to concentrate—is key for an effective coach. All of the case coaches you'll meet in the next chapters demonstrate this ability well.

Be constantly aware of what's going on inside you, the coach. Your emotions when you're coaching are your barometer on how well your needs are getting met. Pay attention to them. Ask yourself, "Am I getting what I want? Am I using control, coercion, or manipulation to get what I want? What am I not getting that I want? Do I need to stop and reflect on the situation? Is how I'm looking at the situation helping or hurting me? Are my total behaviors consistent with what I want?" Your self-awareness is crucial to becoming an effective coach.

Bringing who you are to the coaching process is just as important as the process you use. Again ask yourself, "What do I want this person's 'little voice' to be saying about me right now?"

Getting Started

When learning any new skill, there comes a time to leave the classroom and start experimenting with what you've learned. To help you make that transition, I've prepared a list of some techniques I've found particularly useful in bridging theory and application. These techniques are also demonstrated in the cases that follow so you can see how they are used in real coaching sessions. (Remember these are tips, not a regimented process, to help you overcome your beginner's nervousness.)

> *Tip #1: Start a coaching session.* A common hesitation in starting a coaching conversation is just that: where do I start? I know I want to coach this person but I don't know where to start.

> I find it helpful to start with a self-evaluation question, something as simple as, "Hey Sarah, how's the Wilson project going?" or "Steve, I got some data on rejects and I'd like your thoughts. Got a minute?" Sometimes a simple, "How's it going?" will release a floodgate of evaluations and perceptions, and you're off and running. I'll talk about different approaches, later in this chapter, on how to deal with an employee who is resistant to your attempts to coach.

> *Tip #2: Play both ends of the scale.* As I indicated in Chapter 3, you may have difficulty at times helping an employee identify what she wants. Your direct attempts, such as, "What do you want from your job?" are getting you nowhere. A tip here is to shift to the other arm of the scale. Ask, "What are you getting right now from your job?" and follow up with, "Is that what you want?" This shift in emphasis from, "What do you want?" to evaluating what you're getting may break a logjam in the coaching session.

> *Tip #3: Get focused—encourage self-evaluation with a simple quantification scale.* Getting and staying focused in a coaching session is important, and can be a challenge at

times. If you're hearing a lot of generalities, such as, "The research project is going fine," or you think the employee is being evasive, with comments such as, "I think the task force is going as well as could be expected," here's a powerful focusing technique. Ask the employee to rate, on a scale of one to ten, his perception. You may say something such as, "On a scale of one to ten, one being awful and ten being great, how's the research project coming along?" or "Think about the task force. On a scale of one to ten, one being useless and ten being extremely productive, where would you put the task force?"

Follow up this question with something like, "Is that where you want it to be?" and "What do you think you could be doing to close the gap?" This technique can help focus the session and lead to planning next steps.

Tip #4: Learn from the past. A common coaching opportunity occurs when you see a sudden drop in performance by an employee who has performed well in the past, but for some reason is not achieving at a level you think is possible. An effective technique is to ask the employee to identify a time when her performance was at a higher level and ask her to compare that situation with her current situation.

The dialogue might go something like this: "Beth, it doesn't sound like you're pleased with your performance. Can you remember a time when you felt like you were performing up to your potential?" After a time is recalled, follow up with, "What seems to be different between that time and now?" The ensuing conversation can be rich in identifying more effective behaviors from her past that may be appropriate for use now.

Tip #5: Data avoids arguments and helps you remain a coach. Many personal conflicts and human relationship difficulties on the job stem from two people having different interpretations of the same data. This is a common phenomenon. In coaching, though, these differences can be disastrous and are typically the basis for arguments. My experience is that arguments are not conducive to effective coaching, so here's my tip:

If you find yourself headed for an argument, stop, empathize, and get more data. As an example, if during a coaching session your emotions are running high and you're thinking, "I can't believe how any mortal would be thinking that way," you're probably headed for an argument. Act on this awareness and say something like, "It sounds like you're not at all pleased with Ed's review of your report. Tell me exactly what he said." or "Tell me exactly what he did."

A good way to test if you're getting data versus meaning is to ask, "Could I capture this on a video camera?" "He was really angry," is meaning, not data. "His voice was raised, his face was red, the veins in his neck were sticking out, and he was tearing up my report" is data! The power of mental models is that they help us make conclusions. The role of a coach is to help clarify if the data match the conclusion.

Tip #6: Stay in the coaching process. As you develop your coaching skills, you can usually tell when you're straying from the coaching process. You're sensing resistance, your frustration level begins to rise, the conversation is headed for an argument, and you *want* to use whatever power you have to change the other person!

Realize what's happening is that, under stress, particularly when you're not getting what you want (you probably want more cooperation, agreement, or compliance), you'll tend to use old, familiar responses rooted in stimulus-response. In essence, your scales are out of balance and your best attempt to balance them is to increase the stimulus either directly (control or coercion) or indirectly (manipulation).

If you feel you're headed toward a no-win situation, here's my tip: consider pausing and summarizing what you've heard. Review in specific detail how you understand the other person is viewing the situation. Then, if you still believe *your* point is valid, rephrase what you want.

Pausing and summarizing can do a couple of things. First, by choosing a different behavior (you were frustrated weren't you?) it allows some time for you, the coach, to ask yourself the question, "Am I using coercion, manipulation, or control instead of offering him information and encouraging him to self-evaluate his behavior?" In essence, ask yourself, "Am I coaching or trying to sell my view?"

Secondly, by summarizing what you heard, you can clarify your employee's perceptions with him. You may also change your perception by hearing yourself describe the other's position!

What I try to keep in mind when I coach is, "Is what I'm doing working?" If it is, I keep doing it. If not, trying harder will just increase the resistance I'm feeling. (Remember homeostasis from Chapter 1?)

Use these tips to help you get started in coaching. You may find some work better than others. Hopefully, they'll help you develop your own coaching style. Remember, the coaching process doesn't follow a strict regimen or step-by-step process. There's great value in flexibility.

A Quick Review and Using the Icons in the Demonstrations

Before we get into the case illustrations, I want to review the coaching process and how the icons are used to help you remember each component.

The first principle states that what you want and how you judge the result you're getting is based on your personal interests, attitudes, and values. Remember, we all have six basic values to greater or lesser degrees, and our wants grow out of these values. We'll use a gift to symbolize what the employee wants – something of value to the employee.

Figure 31

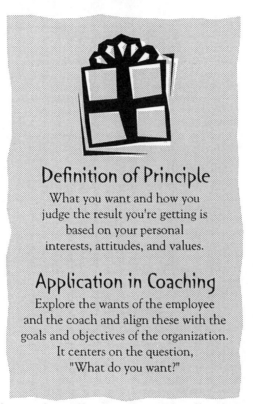

Definition of Principle
What you want and how you judge the result you're getting is based on your personal interests, attitudes, and values.

Application in Coaching
Explore the wants of the employee and the coach and align these with the goals and objectives of the organization. It centers on the question, "What do you want?"

During the coaching illustrations, a gift will indicate that the coach is exploring the wants and needs of the employee.

The second principle tells us that the difference between what you want and what you perceive you're getting is the motivation for all behavior. We've created a scale icon to represent this comparison.

Figure 32

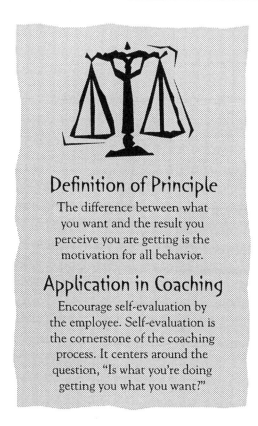

Definition of Principle

The difference between what
you want and the result you
perceive you are getting is the
motivation for all behavior.

Application in Coaching

Encourage self-evaluation by
the employee. Self-evaluation is
the cornerstone of the coaching
process. It centers around the
question, "Is what you're doing
getting you what you want?"

During the coaching illustrations, a scale will indicate the
coach is asking the employee to self-evaluate: 1) what he wants;
2) what he perceives he's getting; or 3) the direction and/or speed
his behavior is taking him.

The third principle of *RealTime Coaching* says that observable
behavior is an attempt to close the gap between what you want
and the result you perceive you're getting. To represent behavior,
we will use an illustration of a director's clapboard.

Figure 33

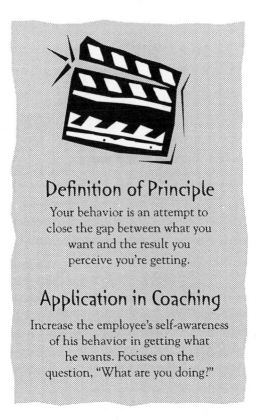

Definition of Principle

Your behavior is an attempt to
close the gap between what you
want and the result you
perceive you're getting.

Application in Coaching

Increase the employee's self-awareness
of his behavior in getting what
he wants. Focuses on the
question, "What are you doing?"

During the coaching illustrations, a clapboard will be used to
indicate when the coach is focusing on the employee's current
behavior or how the employee might want to behave differently
in pursuit of his wants.

The fourth principle states that achieving different results
means either changing what you want or how you behave—both
possible as a result of coaching. Essentially, it means you need to
make a plan; therefore, we have chosen a clapboard icon to represent the planning phase of coaching.

Figure 34

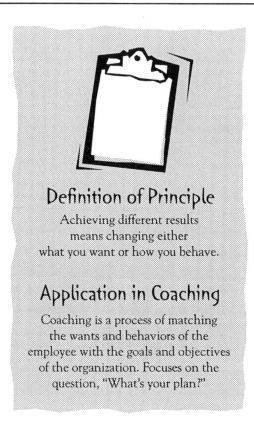

Definition of Principle

Achieving different results
means changing either
what you want or how you behave.

Application in Coaching

Coaching is a process of matching
the wants and behaviors of the
employee with the goals and objectives
of the organization. Focuses on the
question, "What's your plan?"

During the coaching illustrations, the clipboard will signify
when a plan of action is needed.

Here then is the *RealTime Coaching* model:

Figure 35

The RealTime Coaching Model

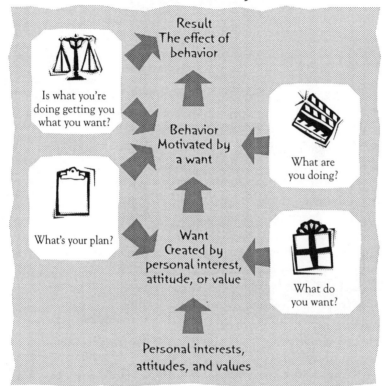

Adapting Your Style for Effective Coaching

Up to this point we've been primarily concerned with "what" the coach says. In the introduction to each of the coaching dialogues in the following four chapters we'll also present tips on "how" to communicate with each person being coached, based on their core behavioral style.

"But how," you ask, "will I know the core behavioral style of someone I'm coaching?" Good question, and here's the answer: Refer back to Chapter 5 and the four groups of words you reviewed to determine *your* core style. Think about the person you will be coaching and select a group of words that *best* describes the person *most* of the time. Identify the core behavioral style associated with the word grouping. Then, review the section in Chapter 5 that describes how to coach the style you selected. This seemingly simple process has proven to be 85% accurate in determining another's core behavioral style.

You also may be asking, "What if I don't have a Personal Interests, Attitudes, and Values profile on the person I'm coaching. Can I still coach them using *RealTime Coaching?*" The answer is "Yes, absolutely!" The Values profile presented in Chapter 3 provides valuable information about what motivates a person and can make your coaching more effective and efficient. If you don't have a Values profile, pay close attention to what a person wants and how their wants align with the six values. Then use the information in Chapter 3 to help you fine tune your coaching. Remember, coaching is about helping a person clarify their wants. The Personal Interests, Attitudes and Values profile is a very useful aid, not a requirement, in the coaching process.

As you progress in your experience and ability as a coach, you will likely want to know more about yourself and the people you're coaching. You may then decide to purchase the profiles for yourself and the people you coach. (Sample profiles are in Appendix A and B.)

Where You're Headed as a Coach

As you read the cases, the four principles of *RealTime Coaching* are interwoven in a dialogue between coach and employee. The intent of the dialogue is to find a more effective way for the employee, coach, and organization to satisfy their needs.

As a coach, *by encouraging self-evaluation*, you present three alternative ways to effect change. Specifically, you can help:

1. Change a *want*.

2. Change the *behavior* being used to pursue the want.

3. Change the *perception* of how results are being viewed.

Keep these options in mind as you read the demonstrations and see how they are used in each.

Before You Read the Case Demonstrations

The following cases use a variety of situations to demonstrate the coaching process. As you read each case, keep in mind that the content is *not* as important as the process being demonstrated. I'm not presenting these cases to illustrate how to solve a particular problem, but to demonstrate a process.

Throughout each case:

- You will eavesdrop on the coach's thought process through boxes labeled *Coach's Thoughts*. The *Coach's Thoughts* help you understand how the theory is being applied in the coaching session.

- Coachnotes (e.g. ①) will provide additional comments at the end of the case and allow for more details.

To maximize the benefit of the cases, I suggest the following:

1. First, review the coach's preparation thoughts and the relevant parts of Chapter 5 on how to coach people with different core behavioral styles.

2. Second, just read the dialogue between coach and employee and ignore the *Coach's Thoughts* and the footnotes.

3. Next, read the *Coach's Thoughts* to better understand how the coach is applying the four principles in the coaching process.

4. Then read the footnote comments for further, more detailed explanation of the coaching session.

5. And lastly, read the *Process* section at the end of the case.

I urge you to read all the cases and not base your interest on the subject matter of an individual case. Great learning can be accomplished by reading and studying each case, regardless of the content discussed.

Chapter 8

Fighting TQM

Nothing could be worse. The evil effect of the Baldrige
guidelines on American business can never be measured.
— Dr. W. Edwards Deming
in his last interview, given to
Industry Week two weeks
before his death.

You've already read *Fighting TQM* in Chapter 1 when I first
introduced the coaching dialogue. As you read this case again,
realize how much you've learned about coaching. See how your
knowledge of Bill's behavioral style makes you a better coach and
how the *RealTime Coaching* model gives you a road map for coaching. *Don't skip this case just because you've already read it once.* Read
how Carol prepared for Bill and how her thoughts (see the
Coach's Thoughts throughout the dialogue) helped keep the conversation on track.

This coaching session takes place at the shipping department.
Carol, the department head (Coach), is having a difficult time
with Bill, one of her team members. Carol and Bill are good
friends, but Bill is resisting the new Total Quality Management
(TQM) program and bad-mouthing all the "measuring and meetings" the TQM program requires.

Carol just received another CRS (Customer Rejected
Shipment) from a long-time customer. In fact, several customer
rejects can be directly traced to Bill's inattentiveness on the job.
Due to the continuous manufacturing process, Bill's crew is the

last to inspect the final product. Carol wants Bill to be more careful in releasing shipments to customers, a job he has done competently for more than ten years. Carol thinks the problem is in
their manufacturing process, but Bill is unwilling, up to now, to
cooperate.

Carol is going to try a different approach this time. She
reviews the word groupings in Chapter 5 and determines that Bill
is a Core C. Here is a review of the unique characteristics and
potential blindspots of this core style.

Figure 36

Unique Characteristics and Potential Blindspots of the Core C (Compliant) Behavioral Style

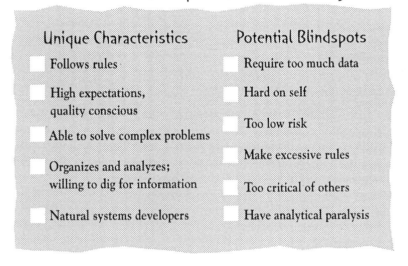

Unique Characteristics	Potential Blindspots
Follows rules	Require too much data
High expectations, quality conscious	Hard on self
Able to solve complex problems	Too low risk
Organizes and analyzes; willing to dig for information	Make excessive rules
Natural systems developers	Too critical of others
	Have analytical paralysis

In reviewing these characteristics Carol quickly realizes that
Bill's past success has been due to his quality consciousness and
ability to organize and develop efficient systems and procedures
for the shipping operation. She also notes Bill's tendency to blame
others in a critical way is common for this behavioral style and he
will probably resist change unless the benefits are well documented.

Carol then reviews how to coach the Core C style:

- The Core C likes things straightforward and direct. Don't be too casual and informal.

- Be thoughtful. Consider all sides of an issue. Don't force the Core C into quick decisions.

- Present the Core C with specifics. Remember, they like data and information. And don't be vague about your expectations.

- Although you should draw up an action plan in all coaching situations, it's especially important with the Core C. Core C's like dates and milestones.

- If you disagree with a Core C, make sure you have the facts to back you up. Opinions and feelings won't cut it with the Core C.

- Give Core C's time to make decisions. Be careful of trying to "close" with the Core C. He needs time to weigh the facts and make his decision. Also, be careful about physical closeness with the Core C. Core C's like a little space.

With the CRS forms in hand—combined with her knowledge of Bill's strengths, blindspots, and how to adapt her style for effective communication—Carol goes out to the dock to talk with Bill.

> Coach's Thoughts: *I want to set the stage by focusing on the problem, not blaming or finding fault, and asking for help.*

Coach: Hey, Bill, got a minute? I need your help.

Bill: Sure, Carol, what's up?

> Coach's Thoughts: *I'll begin by making him aware of
> a problem and asking if he has any ideas on how to
> prevent this problem in the future (thinking behavior).
> I'm also indirectly assessing his desire to help.*
>
>

Coach: I just got another CRS, I'd like to know what you think
             needs to be done to prevent this from happening in the
             future.

Bill: (*Sarcastically*) I think we ought to call a meeting and
             start measuring something.

> Coach's Thoughts: *Bill's emotional response indicates
> his scales are out of balance. He's not getting some-
> thing he wants. I'll acknowledge his frustration, but I
> won't condone it as effective behavior by discussing it.
> I'll also try again to see if he's interested in helping.* ①
>
>

Coach: Naw, I think we've had enough meetings around here. I
             wonder what you think we need to do to prevent this
             from happening again.

Bill: C'mon, Carol, the pressure to "ship it today" is incredi-
             ble. We have five fewer crew members since the down-
             sizing. All we do anymore is "meet and measure," and

I'm supposed to do the work of three. We go to these quality meetings and talk, draw, and measure. A waste of time, in my opinion. What do you think?

Coach's Thoughts: *His scales are really tipped. He's dealing with his frustration by bad-mouthing the TQM program. I don't think a discussion on the merits of TQM would be helpful. I'll tell him how I see the current situation and try to refocus by asking if he wants to help.②*

Coach: I think we have a problem shipping unacceptable product and it's jeopardizing a good long-term customer relationship. I came out here to see if we could solve the problem. I need to know from you whether or not you're interested in helping me.

           (Long pause)

Bill: Look, Carol, I see product coming off the line that I know doesn't meet our standards. But what I'm hearing from above is "things are tight... work harder... get it out today... run the machines faster." I'm in a bind, caught between a rock and a hard place.③

Coach's Thoughts: *Bill's really frustrated. I'll acknowledge his frustration and see if he wants to help.*

Coach: Yeah, I can see your dilemma. Tell me, if we could work out a way to improve the quality, would that make your job easier?

Bill: You bet. Those machine operators need to know the quality they're producing. You know as well as I, the humidity in here and the temperature outside both affect the machines. I'd like to have a dollar every time I've told them product is bad. It's getting so they hate to see me coming. So, I pass it through, just like them.

Coach's Thoughts: *Bill is giving me his perception. If we blame the problem on the machine operators, I'll get nowhere with Bill. I want to know if Bill wants to be viewed the way he just portrayed himself.*④

Coach: Gee, Bill, that doesn't sound like the type of employee you want to be—one who just passes it through.

Bill: Heck, no. But what can I do?

Coach's Thoughts: *I'll take this as Bill's willingness to help. Let's see if he has any ideas.*

Coach: That's exactly what I'd like to figure out. You've been here a long time. Is there anything you've been thinking about that could be done better if you just had more support?

Bill: Well, by the time I get product here, the horse is
            already out of the barn. I mean, the product either is or
            is not acceptable. The operators need to know sooner
            in the run to make adjustments.

Coach's Thoughts: *Good idea. Now we're getting
someplace. I'll push a little harder.*

Coach: So, if the operators knew sooner, they could make cor-
            rections. Is there anything you could do to make them
            aware of what's going on?

Bill: I'm not telling them anymore. I'm sure they've heard
            enough from me. They just won't cooperate with me.

Coach's Thoughts: *I'm going to ask Bill to evaluate
this situation and its impact on our customers.*

Coach: So, they're tuning you out. How is their lack of cooper-
            ation affecting our customers?

Bill: You've got the rejects there in your hand. Not very
            good, in my opinion.

Coach's Thoughts: *I'm going to ask Bill to evaluate this situation and its impact on our company and profit sharing.*

Coach: How do you think the customer rejects are affecting our company and the profit sharing plan?

Bill: I'm sure it's not doing us any good.

Coach's Thoughts: *I wonder if Bill has any personal responsibility here?*

Coach: How is their lack of cooperation affecting you?

          (*Pause*)

Bill: It's making my life miserable! So, why don't you talk to them? They're the problem.

Coach's Thoughts: *Bill's scales are clearly out of balance, but he still sees it as their problem. I'll offer another interpretation and ask him to evaluate.*

Coach: I may do that. You've identified some good points for
            improving quality. But for now, it sounds like this situa-
            tion is affecting product quality and customer satisfac-
            tion, and you're miserable.⑤

Bill: Well, I guess you could look at it that way.

> Coach's Thoughts: *Bill is starting to change the way
> he's been looking at the situation. Let's see if this new
> perception opens up any avenues for new behaviors.*

Coach: So, what do you think we need to do?

Bill: I guess I could try once more and see if we could work
            on a way to tell them they're producing substandard
            product. My hunch is they won't listen.

> Coach's Thoughts: *Bill is still unsure. I'll test future
> behavior and ask for his evaluation.*

Coach: Look, let's say you did try once more and they didn't
            listen. Would you be any worse off than you are now?

Bill: No, I guess not.

Coach's Thoughts: *I think we're close to some action
steps. I'm going to push Bill to start developing a plan.*

Coach: You're right, Bill, there does need to be better commu-
          nication between you and the machine operators. How
          might that happen?

Bill: I hate to say this, but we do need a meeting with you,
          me, and the foreman of the machine operators to dis-
          cuss this situation.

Coach's Thoughts: *Good idea. I'll collaborate on this
approach.*

Coach: Yeah, I think you're right. I'd like to arrange that. In
          the meantime could you jot down the items you'd like
          covered in the meeting? Then I'll prepare a very short
          (*smiling*) agenda.

Bill: Sure, I think I can handle that.

Coachnotes

Here are some additional comments to help you better understand the *Coach's Thoughts*.

① Bill's sarcastic response is an attempt to engage Carol in a conversation about the TQM program. It may also be Bill's attempt to avoid addressing the real problem of the CRS's, a common approach for this core behavioral style when potential personal conflict might be encountered. If Carol discusses his frustration, it could be interpreted by Bill as implicit approval of his behavior—that sarcastic remarks are an effective way of communicating—or it would have sidetracked away from handling the CRS's. By indirectly agreeing with him on the meetings, Carol acknowledged Bill's frustration and immediately restated her intent (and ignored Bill's sarcasm).

② The emotional energy in Bill's statements may tempt the coach to argue, refute, or start defending the TQM program. It may also lure the coach away from discussing the CRS's. Since he's asking Carol what she thinks, Carol uses the opportunity to steer the session back to problem solving and away from blaming. Carol effectively ignores Bill's bait because she realizes that the criticism is a blindspot for this core behavioral style.

③ By empathizing with Bill, Carol demonstrates she understands, but does not agree with, Bill's predicament. She also remembers that quality consciousness—a characteristic of Bill's behavioral style—is being threatened. Bill is softening because he is being listened to in a non-judgmental way.

④ Careful attention to offhand comments can pay dividends. Here, Bill's frustration is showing. His emotions indicate unbalanced scales. Carol's hunch is Bill wants to produce quality products, but the system is getting in the way. Carol's comment tries to focus Bill's attention

on what he wants, what he can do, and the fact that
Carol is there to help him.

⑤ Not accepting responsibility for one's situation is a common problem encountered in coaching. Bill has repeatedly acted ineffectively in getting his needs met. When
Carol gets close, Bill points his finger elsewhere. She
also reminds herself that conflict is typically avoided by
the Core C. By Carol agreeing with him on his observations, Bill feels heard. Summarizing the situation in a
questioning tone helps Bill connect in his own mind
that he's responsible for what he's getting.

Processing "Fighting TQM"

This case illustration is a good example of the difficulty
encountered in implementing a major improvement initiative—in
this instance, TQM— and how to effectively coach for a change
in behavior.

The resistance Carol is encountering is a common, albeit ineffective, consequence of Bill's out-of-balance scales. There are two
typical responses to a hostile employee: avoid at all costs, or confront and fight. Coaching gives you a third alternative.

In terms of what we know about human behavior:

1. Bill is clearly in a mismatch situation. What Bill wants
    is to produce quality, get Carol off his back, and have
    the machine operators cooperate. What he perceives
    he's getting is pressure from the top to ship faster, fewer
    people to help him, and, in his opinion, useless meet-
    ings.

2. He's responding to the mismatch by bad-mouthing the
    TQM program, shipping inferior product, and blaming
    his problems on the machine operators.

A key to this case is understanding that Bill's desire to make a
contribution, his inherent quality consciousness, and his desire to
feel productive and useful is being threatened by the TQM program. He feels the pressure of "ship it today," five fewer crew

members, and a management that just wants to "meet and measure." Bill's need to feel worthwhile can be met in only one way:
someone has to be willing to listen to him.

Listening to Bill is a particularly difficult task because of his
sarcasm. As a coach, Carol did not let Bill's ineffective behavior—
sarcasm, blaming, finger-pointing—lure her into an argument. As
a result, she avoided being judgmental in her responses, coercive
in her tone, and controlling in her suggestions. In other words,
she just listened and kept focused on the task at hand.

The need to feel worthwhile—and Bill is a good example—is
one of the strongest and most compelling desires employees bring
to the workplace. In reality, and I will stress it again, there is only
one way this need can be satisfied: *someone has to be willing to listen.*

There are three levels of listening—understanding, agreeing,
and accepting—that will satisfy a person's desire to be recognized
and feel worthwhile.

1. The first is, listen with the intent to *understand*. Being
   able to fully understand how another is experiencing a
   situation is a powerful need-satisfying skill. Many times
   this form of listening is overlooked out of fear that the
   employee will misinterpret the coach's listening as tacit
   agreement or approval. Demonstrating through your
   conversation that you understand how they're seeing it
   is a potent empathic ability.[1]

2. Second, if appropriate, *agree* with the employee.
   Agreement, when sincere and authentic, is a powerful
   need-satisfying gesture. It also allows the dialogue to
   naturally progress to the next step: now that we agree,
   what should we do about it?

3. And third, *accept* the employee's thoughts, ideas, and
   suggestions. It satisfies an employee's desire to feel
   worthwhile when his ideas become standard operating
   procedure.

Carol knew she'd be in for a tough dialogue. Her skillful listening is an important reason for the successful coaching session. Examples of Carol demonstrating the three levels of listening are:

1. Understanding: "Yeah, I see your dilemma." And, "So, if the operators knew sooner, they could make corrections." And, "So, they're tuning you out."

2. Agreeing: "Naw, I think we've had enough meetings around here." And, "You're right Bill, there does need to be better communication between you and the machine operators."

3. Accepting: "Yeah, I think you're right, I'd like to arrange that."

Footnote

[1] While it is outside the scope of this book to detail listening skills, an excellent description of empathetic listening can be found in *The Seven Habits of Highly Effective People*, 1989, by Dr. Stephen R. Covey.

Chapter 9

The Sales Manager as Coach

Focus, Daniel san. Focus.

—Mr. Miyagi in The Karate Kid

In this situation, the sales manager, Nancy (Coach), has noticed a sudden drop in the performance of one of her better sales associates, Sally. Sally has been with the company for several years and has always performed in the top third of the sales force. Nancy has also noticed that Sally is not as conscientious in returning customer calls and following through on the leads given to her. In fact, her previous quarter's performance placed her in the bottom quarter of all sales associates in the office.

Nancy has asked Sally to meet with her to discuss her recent performance. Prior to the meeting Nancy reviews the word groupings in Chapter 5 and determines that Sally is a Core D. Here is a review of the unique characteristics and potential blindspots of this core style.

Figure 37

Unique Characteristics and Potential Blindspots of the Core D (Dominant) Behavioral Style

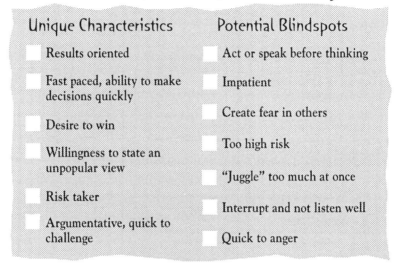

Unique Characteristics	Potential Blindspots
Results oriented	Act or speak before thinking
Fast paced, ability to make decisions quickly	Impatient
	Create fear in others
Desire to win	
	Too high risk
Willingness to state an unpopular view	"Juggle" too much at once
Risk taker	Interrupt and not listen well
Argumentative, quick to challenge	Quick to anger

In reviewing these characteristics Nancy quickly realizes that Sally's past sales success has been due to her bottom-line orientation and competitiveness. She also notes Sally's tendency to "over commit" and try to accomplish too much, which is common for this behavioral style. Nancy wonders if Sally might be too involved in other activities. Nancy also mentally notes that Sally's temper may flair as it has done in the past.

Nancy then reviews how to coach the Core D style and reads from Chapter 5 that, "In communicating, Core D's are direct, to the point. They may come across as blunt or impolite." She reminds herself not to let Sally's directness overly concern her. In addition, here's what Nancy reviews as the tips on how to coach Sally:

• Be clear, specific, and to the point. Stick to business. Don't ramble or make small talk; a Core D will become impatient.

- Come prepared. The Core D wants things in a well-organized package of logically presented facts. Remember: don't waste their time.

- Ask specific questions, not rhetorical ones. Core D's prefer "what" questions.

- If you disagree with a Core D, take issue with the facts, not the person. Try not to be offended by the way a Core D argues; instead, focus on the content of the argument.

- Provide an opportunity for a win/win situation. Don't force the Core D into a losing position. They hate losing.

Here's the dialogue of the meeting.

> Coach's Thoughts: *I want to start by seeing if Sally is concerned about her performance and how she is seeing this meeting.*

Coach: Thanks for stopping by, Sally. As you know, I asked to meet with you to discuss your last quarter's sales performance. When I asked you yesterday if we could meet, what went through you mind?

Sally: It's not what went through my mind, it's what went up and down my spine! I felt like I was going to be called on the carpet.

Coach's Thoughts: *I'm going to restate the perception and check out her concern.*

Coach: Well, quite the contrary. But it sounds like you're concerned about your performance, too. Is that right?

Sally: It's been a tough quarter. We've added three new sales associates, interest rates went up, and it's just plain harder getting an appointment these days. It seems like all I get anymore is voice mail.

Coach's Thoughts: *Sally isn't taking much responsibility for her performance by blaming it on things she can't control. If I address those issues, it will get us off track. I'm going to bypass her comments and show her results of her past behavior.*

Coach: I see. I've taken the liberty of graphing your performance by quarter for the last three years. Tell me what you see going on. (*Hands Sally the graph.*) ①

Sally: Wow, I didn't think I was doing that badly.

Coach's Thoughts: *Sally's surprise indicates an out-of-balance situation. I'm going to try to get her to evaluate her performance.*

Coach: Sally, why do you think you had such a sudden drop in performance this past quarter?

Sally: Well, like I said, interest rates, new sales associates, and...

Coach's Thoughts: *Bad question. It allowed her to blame things outside her control. I'm going to try to be more direct and have her evaluate her behavior.②*

Coach: Let me ask it another way, Sally. Can you think of anything you're doing differently this past quarter that might account for the change?

Sally: Are you saying I'm not trying? You know I'm one of the hardest workers around here. Selling doesn't come all that easy to me, but it's a real challenge that I love.

> Coach's Thoughts: *She's interpreting this question as a criticism. I don't want to argue. It will get us nowhere. I need to be more specific with my intentions.*

Coach: There's no question that you're trying, Sally. And I know you're very dedicated. What I'm trying to uncover is what has been different this past quarter.

Sally: I don't know. I can't think of anything. Look, everybody's down, right?

> Coach's Thoughts: *She's still not focusing on her behavior. I'm going to give her more data and ask her to evaluate her efforts.*

Coach: We've had a slight drop in overall company sales, but I'm most interested in your situation. Your performance dropped from a consistent top third placement to the lower third.

Tell me, how would you compare your effort during this past quarter with the quarter last year when you won the sales achievement award?③

Sally: Boy, everything fell into place that quarter. We got the new computer system that helped me track leads and reminded me when I needed to call back. It even kept me honest on the number of calls I made each week and plotted them against my goals. I used the system religiously.

> Coach's Thoughts: *Good, Sally, now evaluate what you just said. I want you to become more aware of what you are doing.*
>
>

Coach: So, you were working a plan, had some goals, and were tracking your performance. Do you think that effort paid off for you?

Sally: Absolutely! I'm very proud of the sales achievement award.

> Coach's Thoughts: *Good, Sally. Now continue to evaluate what you just said.*
>
>

Coach: What about now, Sally, compared to when you were setting goals, using the system, and tracking your performance? If the quarter you won the sales award your effort was a ten, how would you evaluate your effort now from one to ten?④

          (Brief silence as Sally ponders the question.)

Sally: A four.

Coach's Thoughts: *I need to know what Sally's goals are, and is a four what she wants?*

Coach: A four. Is that acceptable to you?

Sally: No. But I don't think I could give a ten all the time.

Coach's Thoughts: *Now we're getting someplace. Let's see if she's willing to set a goal.*

Coach: What do you think would be a realistic goal for you?

Sally: I'd like to target at least a seven each quarter.

Coach's Thoughts: *Evaluate your goal for me, Sally.*

Coach: And if you did a seven, do you think that would be enough to place you in the upper third where you have been performing?

Sally: Yeah, I think it would.

Coach's Thoughts: *Let's get down to some specific planning.*

Coach: Good. What do you think you need to do now to get
         you from a four to a seven? Are you using the contact
         tracking system now, like you did before?

Sally: Well, kind of. I've been real busy lately. We just bought
         a house and I volunteered for PTA. And entering all
         that data after each call is time consuming.

Coach's Thoughts: *I want you to evaluate what you just said in terms of getting you where you want to go.*

Coach: So you have a lot more going on in your life now. Tell
         me, do you think if you used the contact tracking sys-
         tem like you did before it would help you make better
         use of your time or hamper your effectiveness?

Sally: (*Smiling*) Okay, okay, I hear you! You're right. I really
         haven't used the system the way I used to.

Coach's Thoughts: *I wonder if Sally wants anything from me?*

Coach: Sally, what can I do to help you?⑤

Sally: That data and graph you had on my performance was very…revealing. Do you do that for all the sales associates? Because I'd sure like to review my performance more often.

Coach's Thoughts: *Great! A little more specific and I think we have it!*

Coach: Sally, what would you like in the way of specific information? The system is pretty flexible. I can get most anything you want.

Sally: I'd like to see the graphs each month. And I'd like the graph you prepared on me and the data from the quarter I won the sales achievement award. I'll set that as a ten and see what I need to do to improve.

Coach's Thoughts: *Okay! Let's collaborate on a plan.*

Coach: Tell you what: if I prepare this data for you, will you
         draw up a short-term plan, say for the next two
         months, on what your weekly goals are?

Sally: Sure.

> Coach's Thoughts: *I want to check to see if her anxi-
> ety level about this meeting has diminished.*

Coach: Tell me, Sally, do you think you've been " called
         on the carpet?"⑥

Sally: No, I feel a lot better already.

> Coach's Thoughts: *I want to be sure we both agree
> on next steps and also propose a follow up.*

Coach: Good. Do you think it would be helpful for us to get
         together and review your progress weekly for the next
         couple of weeks? Our first meeting could be this Friday
         and we can go over your short-term plan. What do you
         think?

Sally: I'll be here. Thanks, Nancy, for being so patient with
         me.

Coachnotes

Here are some additional comments to help you understand the Coach's Thoughts better.

① Using data is a powerful tool in coaching. It focuses the coaching dialogue on results and away from judging the person. Using data, rather than opinion, allows Sally to critically evaluate her behavior and the results she's achieving. It also shows Nancy is prepared, and by asking a "what" question demonstrates she is adapting to Sally's Core D style.

② Hey, nobody's perfect, but it demonstrates a point. We all have a "story" (read: excuses) on why we don't get the results we wanted. In fact, most of our reasons blame some external event, another person, or an act of God. But you rarely hear, "I really was lazy and didn't follow up very well on my leads, nor was I very persistent in follow up." The point here is that "why" questions are rarely effective in encouraging self-evaluation. Usually there is an automatic response to be protective and defensive. The reason? Because "why" questions are usually interpreted as external and judgmental evaluation of performance.

③ A powerful coaching technique is having Sally identify a time when she felt successful, because the past situation is a time when her behaviors were working for her. It's also a good specific—not rhetorical—question that is preferred by the Core D. The comparison Nancy asked her to make helps her become more aware of what she was doing effectively then that might be used in the present situation.

④ Quantitative comparisons are extraordinarily useful tools for the coach and appreciated by this behavioral style. The comparison Nancy asked Sally to make will help her evaluate her current effort against a benchmark.

⑤ Reminding Sally that Nancy is here to help, and wants her to succeed, is an important message that demonstrates Nancy's "do with" approach to relating. The message clearly positions Nancy as an ally, not a boss, and lays the groundwork for a productive short-term plan.

⑥ Nancy remembers that Core D's hate losing and want win/win situations. Here, Nancy is checking to see if Sally found the meeting helpful. More times than not, the session should end on a positive note: something is going to be different and better in the future.

Processing "The Sales Manager as Coach"

I hope you're beginning to realize the "RealTime" decisions a coach has to make and the level of concentration required to be effective. In this case, and the previous one, the coach is:

Constantly processing what the employee is saying through the four principles of *RealTime Coaching*, asking:

- What is tipping Sally's scales?

- What does she want that she's not now getting?

- How is she looking at her situation? Is it helping her?

- Is Sally aware she is choosing her behaviors?

- Are Sally's behaviors effective in getting her what she wants?

Asking, "Where do I want to guide this conversation, what do I want, and how can I construct a question that will:"

- Help Sally become more aware of what she's "doing"?

- Encourage her to evaluate the effectiveness of her behaviors?

- Help Sally make better decisions and choose

behaviors that result in getting her more of what she wants *and* more sales for the company?

Thinking "What should I do next to get what I want?"

As you've seen, to keep the session on track, the coach may at times ignore or acknowledge, but not discuss, what an employee is telling him or her.

The Sales Manager as Coach is also a good illustration of two powerful coaching techniques that increase an employee's awareness of their *doing* behavior:

1. The first is the use of data.

   The coach's preparation of data (graphing Sally's performance by quarter for the past three years and showing her ranking with other sales associates) is "clear, specific and to the point"—an approach that is preferred by this core behavioral style. It also gave Sally a vivid picture of her performance, probably far better than any qualitative management evaluations or other comparisons. By allowing Sally to evaluate what the data meant to her, the coach was reinforcing a nonjudgmental and supportive position.

2. The second is the use of comparisons with simple quantifications.

   Making historical comparisons is an extremely useful technique that encourages self-evaluation by the employee. Examples are when Nancy said to Sally, "Tell me, how would you compare your effort during this past quarter with the quarter last year when you won the sales achievement award?" And asking for placements on a simple scale such as, "If the quarter you won the sales award your effort was a ten, how would you evaluate your effort now from one to ten?" Here, Sally becomes painfully aware of her effort (a four), her behavior, and her sales performance by responding to two simple comparison questions. The resulting dialogue reveals Sally's goals and aspirations for the future.

Chapter 10

What To Do When What You're Doing Isn't Working

---

accountability: A characteristic of which everyone else
   in the organization needs far more. Not to be confused
   with Authority (see below), which is what I need
   more of.
authority: A characteristic of which I need more if I am
   to do my job properly. Not to be confused with
   Accountability (see above), which is what everyone
   else in the organization needs far more of.
                        — Eileen Shapiro
                        Fad Surfing in the Boardroom

   This next case demonstrates that coaching situations can present themselves in a number of unexpected ways. It also illustrates
that you may not have time to adequately prepare for a coaching
conversation. My tip is this: Begin now identifying the core
behavioral styles of each of the people you now manage or super-
vise. Learn their unique characteristics and potential blindspots
and begin relating with them on a "do with" basis by adapting
your style for more effective communication.

   In this example, Rick works for Blake (coach). They've been
working together on a major project that is quickly coming to a
close. Deadlines are pressing and tempers are a little short. Blake
also knows Rick is having a difficult time getting some needed
information from a coworker, Al. Blake knows Al's core behavioral style is an S and Rick's is a D. Before you read the case,
review the unique characteristics, potential blindspots and coaching tips for both the Core D and Core S styles found in Chapter 5

and see if you can determine what the problem might be between Rick and Al. (After the dialogue, we'll discuss how these two different behavioral styles can cause relationship problems if not understood and accepted.)

Rick just happens to stop by Blake's office to let off some steam about the lack of cooperation he's experiencing from Al. Let's join them.

Rick: Man, I just got my head chewed off by Al. I've been trying to get the account information from him for the report I owe you and he's sandbagging me. Telling me he doesn't have time, he'll get to it tomorrow, blah, blah, blah... I can't trust him. So today I asked him where it was, and he went ballistic.

Coach's Thoughts: Rick's scales are really unbalanced. He needs the report, but Al's being a rascal. Let me see if I can refocus the discussion.

Coach: And it sounds like you still don't have the report?

Rick: Right. I don't know what to do. Will you talk to him? Or better yet, talk to his boss, and tell him Al has to cooperate?

Coach's Thoughts: Rick's not focusing on what he might be able to do. I don't want to intervene. They should be able to work things out. I wonder what Rick has done so far about getting the report.①

Coach:	You sound really frustrated. Tell me exactly what you've done with Al up to this point.

Rick:	Well, after I got the assignment from you, I wrote him a memo saying I needed the account information from him by Friday. That was two weeks ago.

> Coach's Thoughts: *Sounds normal to me, but that doesn't really matter. It didn't work. I'll explore more specific behaviors.*②

Coach:	Do you have a copy of the memo?

Rick:	Sure. Here it is.

> Coach's Thoughts: *Let me see if Rick can help by evaluating the memo.*

Coach:	*(Reads memo out loud to Rick.)* How did your memo sound when I read it out loud?

Rick:	All right, I guess… maybe a little demanding. I was in a hurry wrapping up the Wilson project and maybe it showed.

Coach's Thoughts: *I wonder what Rick's perception is of Al.*

Coach: Do you think your being in a hurry showed to Al?

Rick: I don't know.

Coach's Thoughts: *I'll restate the question.*

Coach: How do you think Al might have taken your memo?

Rick: Are you saying I've got to sugar-coat all my requests? Why can't Al just cooperate and give me the info I need?

Coach's Thoughts: *Rick's interpreting this as criticism. I'll reframe the thought and see if it helps.*

Coach: Rick, I'm not asking you to do anything you don't want to do.③ But I've got to say that what you have done hasn't gotten you the report.

Rick: You're right about that.

Coach's Thoughts: *Good. Let's get back to what was done.*

Coach: What did you do next?

Rick: Well, Friday came and went. Monday, first thing, I went to Al's office and asked him if he got the memo I sent him on the account information I needed. He said, "Yeah, it's here somewhere." And then he kind of ignored me. I've got to admit I was more than a little miffed when we talked. I mean, our deadline was closing in on me.

Coach's Thoughts: *I want to check out whether Al even read Rick's memo.*

Coach: Do you think he read the memo?

Rick: Oh, he read it all right.

Coach's Thoughts: *Rick needs to evaluate what Al's behavior is saying.*

Coach: What is Al's behavior telling you?

Rick: We go back a long way. We don't have a great relation-
           ship, but nothing like this. He's sure upset about some-
           thing and I'm taking the brunt of it.

Coach's Thoughts: *I'm going to press a little harder here.*

Coach: It also sounds like Al doesn't want anything to do with
           you right now. And you're paying the price. What do
           you think is going on between you two?

Rick: Well, ever since my promotion, I've been a bit edgy
           and impatient with others. Even my kids are telling me
           to "chill out." Maybe I'm coming across as too demand-
           ing and this is Al's way of putting me in my place.

Coach's Thoughts: *I'll clarify what I just heard.*

Coach: You may be right. I don't know what Al's thinking. But
           I know under the present circumstances he's not about
           to give you the information you need.

Rick: Yeah, you're probably right... Well, thanks for the help.
           I'll think about what you said.

Coach's Thoughts: *Whoa! We've got a little more to cover here. I haven't heard anything that would lead me to believe the situation between the two of them is going to change. I wonder what Rick's evaluation is?*

Coach: I'm glad I could be of some help, but tell me, will just thinking④ about what we said help you get the information from Al any quicker?

Rick: What do you mean?

Coach's Thoughts: *I'll be a little more specific here, tell Rick how I see it and ask for an evaluation.*

Coach: You told me you're going to think about what we said. I just want to know if your thinking about it will improve your relationship with Al. It seems to me you're up against a deadline. Tell me what you're going to do and whether thinking about what we said is enough.

Rick: Right now, I don't know. I do know I'll need more time, so I'd like to request an extension of our deadline for one week.

Coach's Thoughts: *Rick's not taking much responsibility here. I need to set a boundary, no extensions. Rick needs to get a better idea of where to go from here.*

Coach: No, I don't think an extension is fair to the other team members. I agree time is tight, but not unreasonable. If you got the information from Al today, could you prepare your part of the project?⑤

Rick: Sure, but Al's not talking to me, remember?

Coach's Thoughts: *Let's go back to the basics here.*

Coach: As it stands now, Rick, what do you want to happen?

Rick: Well, I still need the information from Al. After that, it's downhill. I mean everything else is done.

Coach's Thoughts: *I think we can get to a little planning here.*

Coach: So, if you got the information from Al today, you could
            meet the deadline? What do you think you need to do
            in order to make that happen?

Rick: I have to talk to Al. It's the only chance I have. Maybe
            he'll be more reasonable this time.

Coach's Thoughts: *Seems like a lot is riding on Al's
mood. Let's see how Rick would handle it.*

Coach: If Al were here, what would you say?

Rick: I'd say, "Al, since you haven't given me the informa-
            tion I told you I needed, I'm up against a serious dead-
            line. What are the chances you could get the account
            information for me right now?"

Coach's Thoughts: *Evaluate your behavior, please.*

Coach: What do you think he'd say your chances are?

Rick: He'd say, "Two: slim and none."

Coach's Thoughts: *This is the same tone as the memo!*
Do you really think it would work, Rick?

Coach: Is what you've just said any different from how you
          asked for it before?

Rick: No, not really.

Coach's Thoughts: *Once again. Do you really think it*
would work, Rick?

Coach: But you'd expect a different response from Al, and his
          cooperation, right?

Rick: Hey, it's worth a try. What are you saying?

Coach's Thoughts: *This is the same tone as the memo!*
Do you really think it would work, Rick?

Coach: Rick, what do you think I'm trying to help you realize?
          (Rick pauses and looks around the office.)

Rick: I get it. It's like that plaque says over there on your
          wall, "Craziness is doing the same thing over and over
          but expecting a different result." You're saying I need to
          try something different.

Coach's Thoughts: *Great! I'll share my opinion and see
if Rick sees any new options.*

Coach: Now that would be worth a try. I know Al is basically a
          good guy, and like anybody else feels the daily pressures
          of his job. What do you think you need to change?

Rick: How about I try this: "Al, I think I blew it with you. I
          let my pressures spill over and I think I came across as
          demanding. I'm sorry for the way I've been acting
          toward you about this report. Is there a way we can
          work this out?"⑥

Coach's Thoughts: *Very impressive. Now a little plan...*

Coach: Sounds like it's worth a try. When will you talk with
          Al?

Rick: (*Grinning*) Boy, are you demanding! I'll call him right
          now and see if I can stop over this afternoon.

Coach's Thoughts: ... *and some follow up.*

Coach: Give me a call before you leave today and fill me in on
          how it went, okay?

Rick: Sure, Blake. Thanks for the help.

Coachnotes

Here are some additional comments that will help you understand the Coach's Thoughts better.

① If the coach stepped in, it would absolve both Rick and
    Al of the responsibility to handle their differences, and
    little growth or improvement would happen. By not
    intervening on Rick's behalf, the coach established a
    boundary for acceptable behavior. It also demonstrates
    that Blake is not a "do for" boss.

② Notice Rick's directness and task orientation, which is
    very common with the Core D behavioral style. Also,
    Blake is aware that what makes sense to him may not to
    Rick. This illustrates how fast our mind interprets data
    and assigns meaning, and how important it is to slow
    down and examine the conclusions we make from the
    data we're given.

③ The coach is stating here he is not a "do to"or "do for"
    boss. He won't tell Rick what to do if Rick doesn't want
    to. Plus the Core D style doesn't like to be told what to
    do anyhow! But Blake will have Rick evaluate his cur-
    rent behaviors and where they've gotten him.

④ Many coaching sessions that follow a different model would end here. Our theory states that nothing will change unless a "doing" behavior changes. Just thinking about something rarely changes anything. Also, this is a good illustration of Core D's impatience and impulsiveness to get going whether or not they have a good plan.

⑤ Again, a boundary is established, which is what the coach wants. See the following section on processing this case for more on boundary-setting in coaching.

⑥ Blake knows that Rick's directness may be offensive to Al's Core S style. By relating to Al as a "person" not just as a "task," Rick will probably succeed in getting better cooperation. Also, this turnaround in Rick's communication style may seem a bit unrealistic. In reality, the coach may "role play" with Rick several times before he comes up with this approach.

Processing "What To Do When What You're Doing Isn't Working"

This case is a good example of how Blake, the coach, helped Rick become more self-aware of his total behavior. Rick was very aware of his feelings toward Al, and he knew what he needed to complete for his part of the project. However, he was unaware of his outward behavior—how he acted—and his treatment of Al, and how that influenced Al's behavior toward him.

It may have been tempting for Blake to silently read Rick's memo and comment on how it might have seemed demanding. By avoiding this external evaluation, Blake got Rick to self-evaluate and become more aware of how his behavior was affecting Al.

Another key point is Blake's persistence on a plan that would include doing something different, not just thinking about the situation. At first, this may seem awkward and maybe a bit pushy. If you get to the planning stage in a coaching session and you get resistance, do what Blake did and ask for an evaluation. Ask, in essence, "If you don't do what you are resisting doing, will it help you?"

The case also illustrates the use of boundaries in a coaching session. Setting and adhering to boundaries can be explained and understood at three levels in an organization:

1. First, there are interpersonal boundaries, the stated and unstated rules that govern human interactions. These include common courtesies and extend to include customs and culturally accepted norms of relationships.

2. Second, there are departmental boundaries. These are the rules and procedures that govern the operation of a department or unit within an organization. These boundaries typically include hours of operation, dress code, and the desires and idiosyncrasies of the department manager.

3. The third level of boundaries is organizational, the culture, or norms of behavior, acceptable for all employees.

Several examples of boundaries can be found in this case: first when Blake said, "I'm not asking you to do anything you don't want to do," and second, when he refused to grant an extension to Rick's deadline request. Both statements clearly define what Blake will and won't do. When he refused the extension, he proceeded to check out his perception that the report could be done on time by asking, "If you got the information from Al today, could you prepare your part of the project?" Rick's initial desire to extend the deadline was not so much based on the workload, but more to avoid confronting Al.

This last comment pertains to "trying something different." Many times, ineffective behavior is repeated over and over again with the hope that something different will result. (You may have experienced this phenomenon if you've ever lost your car keys. How many times did you check and recheck the same places saying, "They've just got to be here!") Blake was very skillful in helping Rick understand he was continuing to use behaviors that had proven ineffective in dealing with Al.

Chapter 11
Gridlock at the Top: The CEO as Coach

A great many people think they are thinking when they are merely rearranging their prejudices.
—William James

Boyd listened intently. It wasn't the first time he'd experienced differences of opinion between manufacturing and marketing. In fact, he thought debate was healthy, as it pushed both sides to rigorously analyze their positions. But this time was different. Mark, the senior VP in charge of sales and marketing, and Scott, the senior VP responsible for manufacturing, were really going at each other. Both were far more aggressive in stating their opinions and vehement in defending their positions than Boyd had experienced before. Boyd was also getting more than a little impatient with the lack of progress in bringing new products to market—something he held Scott and Mark jointly responsible for. What he heard was a lot of bureaucratic excuses. He feared Pioneer was losing its entrepreneurial spirit.

Boyd's company, Pioneer Manufacturing, is hugely successful. The company has grown from one small plant serving the state to five regional locations that serve the entire United States. Mark joined Pioneer about four years ago as VP of Marketing and Sales. Since then, Pioneer has experienced phenomenal growth in both revenues and profits. Mark comes from a consumer packaged goods background with several stints at Fortune 500 companies.

Scott, on the other hand, has been with Boyd since the start, almost 20 years. Scott is the VP of Manufacturing and prides himself in being a "home grown" executive and an innovator in the industry. Both executives are seasoned, and are largely responsible for Pioneer's recent, enviable growth. They both, however, have strong personalities. Scott can be extremely intimidating and condescending at times, and Mark can come off as glib and arrogant.

The current flap between Mark and Scott is about whether Pioneer should drop a particular product from the line. The product is a cash cow, but sales have been declining. Scott wants to milk it further. Mark on the other hand, wants to bury it and free up manufacturing resources for a newer electronic model—a model, he says, competitors will be introducing in twelve to eighteen months.

Boyd knows the rapid growth of his company has stretched everyone's abilities, but this is different. He knows he can't tolerate these skirmishes that have escalated into battles. He also wonders if this is another symptom of a creeping malaise that is killing Pioneer's spirit.

When the action paused, Boyd saw an opening. Calling for their attention, he started, "Mark… Scott… I heard a saying once that went something like this: 'If two are arguing, it's not the issue at hand that's the problem, but the state of their relationship.' I'd like you both to think about the disagreement you're having and look at your relationship. You are both very important executives to Pioneer and friends to me personally. I'd like to meet first thing tomorrow morning—from 8:30 to 9:00 with you, Mark, and from 9:00 to 9:30 with you, Scott. At 10:00, we'll all meet together and see where we are."

That night Boyd identified Mark's core style as an I and Scott's as an S. Here's what he sees as Mark's unique characteristics and potential blindspots.

Figure 37

Unique Characteristics and Potential Blindspots
of the Core I (Influencing) Behavioral Style

Unique Characteristics	Potential Blindspots
Creative problem solver	Talk before thinking
Enthusiastic, natural optimism	Lose track of time, often late and hurried
Humorous	Abandon position in conflict
Fun loving	Disorganized
High contactability, trusting of others	Overly trusting
Ability to make others feel welcome or included	Overly optimistic, can be superficial

Here's what he sees as Scott's unique characteristics and potential blindspots.

Figure 38

Unique Characteristics and Potential Blindspots
of the Core S (Steady) Behavioral Style

Unique Characteristics	Potential Blindspots
Tenacity for order, stability and closure	Possessive of things
Need for secure situations	Too low risk
Great listener, calms and stabilizes others	Hold a grudge
Good planner, natural ability to organize tasks	Too agreeable
Able to mask emotions	Resistant to change
	Too indirect when communicating

Boyd further reviewed the coaching tips on each style and prepared his approach.

At 8:30 the next morning, Mark comes to Boyd's office. After exchanging pleasantries and settling down with a cup of coffee, they start their conversation.

(Note: There are no coachnotes for this case.)

Coach's Thoughts: *I want to find out what Mark thought about our conversation yesterday and how he sees his relationship with Scott.*

Coach: So what did you think about last night? (Boyd)

Mark: You've been pushing us, and rightly so, to speed up our new product introductions. This is a perfect opportunity to do just that. The ten-eighty model is dead, it just hasn't been buried yet. And the longer we wait, the longer we'll be uncompetitive in the marketplace.

Coach's Thoughts: *He's not addressing the relationship, I need to be more specific.*

Coach: I see. How do you see your relationship with Scott?

Mark: It seems like Scott is really getting conservative: checking everything, slow to change. In fact, he's getting harder and harder to talk to. Always finding fault, why something won't work rather than how to make it work.

Coach's Thoughts: *I want Mark to begin looking at the way he acts toward Scott.*

Coach: So you've noticed a change? Has that changed the way you work with him?

Mark: What do you mean?

Coach's Thoughts: *Mark is unaware that he may have changed his behavior toward Scott. I'll ask the question again to determine if Mark can begin to see that he is partially responsible for his relationship with Scott.*

Coach: I mean, have you changed?

Mark: When I first came here, you told me, in your words, that *(smiling)* "Pioneer is a sleeping—maybe even comatose—giant, full of potential." And that marketing had been "sorely neglected." You also said, "We're just a bunch of engineers who don't know anything about marketing or selling." It's been a real struggle at times to convince Scott of the need to market and be responsive to the customer.

Coach's Thoughts: *I'm going to continue asking Mark about his behavior toward Scott.*

Coach: What have you done to convince Scott of the need for marketing?

Mark: I assumed he wanted to grow and make more money. In reality, I couldn't believe his naiveté when it came to marketing. I remember one time I said, "Scotty, you just worry about making it, I'll tell you what the customers want and worry about selling it." *(Laughing.)*

Coach's Thoughts: *I'm starting to see a problem here. Mark needs to evaluate that last statement.*

Coach: Did that help, the division of labor between making and selling?

Mark: You know Boyd, it's hard to teach an old dog new tricks!

Coach's Thoughts: *I need to be clear here that I want him to begin looking at his relationship with Scott. I'm not going to respond to Mark's flippant comment about Scott.*

Coach: I mean, did it change the relationship in any way?

Mark: Yeah, it helped. We didn't talk much after that. (*Grinning.*) Look, in all my experience, I've yet to see anything less than simmering resentment between marketing and manufacturing. It's just the way business is.

Coach's Thoughts: *Let's get a more precise reading on the relationship.*

Coach: Right now Mark, on a scale of one to ten, with one being a "rapid boil of resentment," where would you put your relationship with manufacturing?

         (*Brief pause.*)

Mark: Oh, I'd say a two or three.

Coach's Thoughts: *Let's see if that's what he wants.*

Coach: Is that where you want it?

Mark: That's just the way it is. Scott will simmer down.
            (*Obviously relishing his pun.*) Plus, I wouldn't know what
            to do to cool him off.

> Coach's Thoughts: *I've got a good picture from
> Mark's side.*

Coach: Okay... I know Scott should be here about now.
            Thanks for your time, and I'll see you at 10:00. Oh, but
            before you leave, would you think about one question?
            You don't have to answer it now, just think about it?

Mark: Sure, anything...shoot.

> Coach's Thoughts: *I'm going to try something here to get
> Mark to see his relationship through a different lens.*

Coach: What could we accomplish as a company if your rela-
            tionship with Scott was a ten on your scale, full cooper-
            ation, rather than resentment?

            (*Mark leaves Boyd's office and Scott arrives. After some
            small talk they sit down and start their conversation.*)

> Coach's Thoughts: *Great! I want to find out what Scott
> thought about our conversation yesterday and how he sees
> his relationship with Mark.*

Coach: So what did you think about last night?

Scott: Well, I'm not afraid to say, I didn't get much sleep last
          night. In our 20 years together, Boyd, I've never worked
          with a more arrogant, glib, know-it-all person. I'm at
          the end of my rope as to how to deal with Mark.

Coach's Thoughts: *He's not addressing the relationship. I
need to be more specific.*

Coach: I understand. How have you been dealing with him?

Scott: When he first came here, I wanted us to get off on the
          right foot. I know how you agonized over the decision.
          And I think we did for a while.

Coach's Thoughts: *I wonder if Scott can identify any
changes.*

Coach: For a while? What changed?

Scott: I don't know exactly when, but the more success we
          had, the more he wanted to take all the credit. He kept
          putting his Fortune 500 experience in everybody's face
          like, "You dummies, here's how you do it!"

Coach's Thoughts: *I'll ask him about his behavior toward Mark.*

Coach: So what did you do?

Scott: I ignored him for the most part. I knew where we came
           from and the struggles we faced early on to make a
           buck. Boy, those were the good old days. Now we rarely
           get to just talk. Always a meeting, tight agenda... this
           growth has taken a lot of the fun out of Pioneer.

Coach's Thoughts: *Scott is being very candid here. He misses the closeness we once had. I'll note it and come back to the issue at hand.*

Coach: I'd like to hear more of your observations on fun.
           Maybe we could talk about that over dinner next week
           when we're at the trade association meeting. But for
           now, I'm interested in how you see the future of your
           relationship with Mark.

Scott: Sure, dinner sounds great, let's plan on it. About my
           relationship with Mark...I don't know. I don't even
           know if I want to spend any time on it.

Coach's Thoughts: *I'd like to hear if Scott and Mark ever got along.*

Coach: Really bad, huh? Was there ever a time when your rela-
           tionship with Mark was working?

Scott: Right after he started. We got along great. He didn't
           have any product knowledge and was like a sponge.
           We'd visit each plant and have dinner on the road
           talking about Pioneer's future. I thought we really had a
           catch.

Coach's Thoughts: *Let's get a more precise evaluation of their relationship.*

Coach: How would you characterize your relationship now?
           Say, on a scale of one to ten, a one being terribly
           painful and a ten where it was when Mark first started.

Scott: (*Without a pause.*) A half.

Coach's Thoughts: *I wonder what Scott would like it to be.*

Coach: Pretty low, huh? Tell me, Scott, is that where you want it to be?

Scott: Heck no. But unless he changes, I don't know what I can do.

> Coach's Thoughts: *I've got a good picture from both sides now. We'll go from here.*

Coach: I see. Well, it's almost 9:30. Let's take a short break and reconvene at 10:00. In the meantime, will you consider one more question? You don't have to answer it now, just think about it and we'll talk more at 10:00.

Scott: Sure.

> Coach's Thoughts: *I'm going to try something here to get Scott to look a little closer at his relationship with Mark.*

Coach: What could we accomplish as a company if your relationship with Mark was a ten on your scale, full cooperation, rather than pain?

> Coach's Thoughts: *That was interesting! I have two brilliant executives who can't get along. I know their warring is slowing down decision making and their resentment toward each other is building. When they get together, I want them to critically evaluate the value of their current relationship and where it's headed.*

(At 10:00, Mark and Scott join Boyd in his office.)

Coach: Who'd like to start?

            (After a brief silence, Mark starts.)

Mark: I'll start. We need a decision on the ten-eighty model,
            pronto. As I explained in our meeting, our competitors
            are twelve to eighteen months away from a fully elec-
            tronic model. If we keep producing the ten-eighty, we
            use valuable manufacturing resources making buggy
            whips. You've been pushing us to step up our new prod-
            uct introductions. This is a perfect opportunity to bring
            a new product to market. Let's have a nice wake for the
            outdated product and join the nineties.

Scott: Hold on here. The ten-eighty is still twelve percent of
            our sales volume and eighteen percent of our profits.
            Plus, it's the standard-bearer of Pioneer. Would you like
            your profit sharing cut by eighteen percent next year?

Mark: I'll take an eighteen percent hit next year rather than a
            hundred percent cut in two years when we're an also-
            ran in the marketplace.

Scott: *(Condescendingly.)* Oh ye of little faith.

> Coach's Thoughts: *I need to stay calm and focused here.
> I want them to critically evaluate the value of their current
> relationship and where it's headed.*

Coach: *(Calmly and without regard to what just happened.)* Well,
            it seems like you're both pretty good at sparring, but I
            knew that before this morning. Continuing to argue
            about the ten-eighty is not going to get anybody any-
            where.

            I'd like to hear from each of you about the benefits you

see in continuing on with your relationship in its present condition—without changing anything. Both of you placed a pretty low rating on the current state of your relationship, and I'd like to hear what you're getting from maintaining it at such a low level.

(Long awkward silence.)

Coach's Thoughts: *I hope the silence indicates a great deal of thought about what I just said. I'll prod a little and see if they're ready to say anything.*

Coach: Scott…Mark…How should I interpret your silence?

(Boyd allows a few moments for them to respond. Not hearing anything, he proceeds.)

Coach's Thoughts: *Good, I think they are thinking. I want to share with them how I see their relationship and ask them once more to evaluate.*

I asked each of you before you left our earlier meeting to consider the benefits of an improved working relationship. I want you to carefully consider what I'm about to say. Okay?

(Both nod in agreement.)

You are both vitally important to the future of Pioneer.

Scott, your commitment and dedication to innovation have made contributions to Pioneer that are immeasurable. Mark, you have a gift for understanding customer needs and wants and I'm forever thankful you chose to share it with us here at Pioneer. Your contribution also cannot be measured.

Both of you have demonstrated to me, your employees, our Board of Directors and our shareholders, your individual, and I stress individual, competency. The performance of Pioneer during the past five years speaks for itself.

We, like our competitors, are faced with many new challenges. We're no longer a small company. Our desire to distribute internationally will only magnify the pressures we're feeling today.

What I want to know is, do you think your working relationship and the course you are both on will help or hinder our ability to meet the challenges we'll face in the future?

(Another brief silence, but this time both Scott and Mark are fully present.)

Scott: It sounds like it's time to bury the hatchet.

Mark: Yeah, you're right, maybe we should bury the hatchet—before we bury the ten-eighty!

(All three laugh. The mood has definitely changed.)

Coach's Thoughts: *Good. I want to be sure we all understand what was just said.*

Coach: Am I hearing that both of you want to change? That
            we need to find a more collaborative approach to solv-
            ing our day-to-day problems and creating our future?

Both: (*Nodding with approval.*) Yes.

> Note: A great deal of very open conversation
> ensued. Both Mark and Scott were hesitant at first
> to admit they were jointly responsible for their rela-
> tionship. With Boyd's coaching, each started to
> view the other differently and more positively.
> Mark became aware of his oftentimes glib attitude
> and Scott realized that he can be quite intimidating.
> A major breakthrough was accomplished and all
> three realized how beneficial an open and authentic
> relationship can be. We rejoin them...

Coach's Thoughts: *Let's see if they have any ideas.*

Coach: Okay, how do you think we should go about it?

Mark: I learned a process I've used on occasion that has
            helped me, particularly when I was a green sales man-
            ager. It's called a "Start, Stop, Continue" process. Two
            people who need to work together put their thoughts
            down about the things they want the other to stop
            doing, start doing or continue doing. It's pretty simple,
            but the results can be very helpful and revealing.

Scott: That's interesting. We use a similar approach in process
            improvement on the plant floor. We've added another
            step called "More." Things we need to do more of.

            I'd be willing to give it a try.

Coach's Thoughts: *I'll confirm what I just heard.*

Coach: So what I'm hearing is that you will both write down
           anything you want the other to start doing, stop doing,
           continue doing, and do more of. Do I have it right?

Both: (*Nodding*) Yes.

Coach's Thoughts: *I'd like to see if they'd be interested in
including me.*

Coach: I'd like to add something. I'd like you to include me. It
           would be very helpful for me to hear your opinions on
           how I'm doing. I'd also like to do one for each of you
           from my perspective. Would you agree to this addition?

Mark: Sure, it's fine with me. I'd welcome the chance.
           (*Smiling*) I hope you know what you're in for!

Scott: Fine by me. (*Pauses*) But one question: how candid can
           we be?

Coach's Thoughts: *I can see we still need to work on the trust between all of us. I'll share with them how I see it and set a date for reconvening.*

Coach: That's a good question, and it probably gets to the heart of our relationships. I'll suggest we use this rule of thumb. If you believe the information you're about to give is helpful for the other to know and he can do something about it, put it down. If, after you consider the thought, you find it may be more critical than help-ful, maybe you should just drop it as a bygone or con-sider reframing it into a more useful comment.

Okay, when should we meet again to talk through our opinions?

Scott: I've got an idea. How about if we reserve some time after the association meeting next week? We'll already be on the coast, away from telephones. We can relax and take our time.

Coach's Thoughts: *Are we all together?*

Coach: Sounds good to me. How about you, Mark?

Mark: Let's do it!

Coach: Great. Let's coordinate the arrangements. And gentle-
          men...thanks for your courage.

(Note: There are no coachnotes for this case.)

Processing "Gridlock at the Top: The CEO as Coach"

This case demonstrates three points:

1. How *RealTime Coaching* can be used with more than one
   individual to help focus attention on a relationship.

2. How the process of coaching can be used at top executive levels of an organization.

3. How the age-old conflict between manufacturing and
   marketing can be confronted constructively.

A major challenge facing growing companies is how they
maintain the energy, excitement, and innovation that typically
characterize earlier periods of growth. Pioneer Manufacturing is
facing such a challenge. Boyd's process is worth examining a little
closer.

- First, he clearly set the stage for talking about Mark and
  Scott's relationship by asking them to think about their
  disagreement overnight. He also reassured them by
  telling them how valuable they both were to Pioneer
  and him personally.

- Second, Boyd spoke with each man individually. He
  knew both Scott and Mark's behavioral style liked personal contact and that individual attention from him
  was warranted. Further, by focusing on a time when
  their relationship was working for each, he increased
  awareness for both that a compatible relationship could
  again be achieved. It also gave Boyd time to further
  understand how each was viewing the relationship.

- And finally, Boyd was diligent in keeping focused on
  the relationship. He knew Mark's approach to interpersonal conflict would be to flee from it and Scott's would
  be to tolerate it, yet do little to change. The discussion
  could have very easily shifted into talking about the
  pros and cons of discontinuing the ten-eighty model.
  His statement asking both to evaluate the benefits of
  continuing an adversarial relationship was a key turning
  point.

Boyd was astute in recognizing that the future of Pioneer is
directly related to the competency and quality of the relationships
of its top executives. His ability to empathetically focus on their
relationship is key to breaking the gridlock experienced in many
organizations.

Chapter 12

Becoming a RealTime Coach

Nothing in the world can take the place of persistence. Talent will not; nothing is more common than unsuccessful men with talent. Genius will not; unrewarded genius is almost a proverb. Education will not; the world is full of educated derelicts. Persistence and determination alone are omnipotent.

— Calvin Coolidge

We tried hard...but it seemed that every time we were beginning to form up into teams we would reorganize. I was to learn later in life that we tend to meet any new situations by reorganizing; and a wonderful method it can be for creating the illusion of progress while producing confusion, inefficiency and demoralization.

—Petronius Arbiter, 210 B.C.

We are just beginning to understand how to create enduring organizations that can compete in a global economy. Our history has not been good. The turmoil, anguish, and disarray caused by downsizing, right-sizing, re-engineering, and massive reorganization seen in many large organizations is our tribute to trying to find a better way.

Current literature is flooded with suggestions, anecdotes, and hyperbole that tingle our senses, but do little to ease the pain. In the cold hard light of day, it's still leader and follower, boss and subordinate, manager and employee, operating in the "last three feet" of human relationships. I hope Peter Drucker was wrong when he recently stated that organizations are being managed by people who "use 90% of their time making it difficult for workers to do their jobs." Managers and leaders at all levels are groping for tools and techniques that will better equip them for the future. I hope *RealTime Coaching* has struck a responsive chord, and provides you with the "how" to truly unleash the power of your people.

How To Begin Implementing RealTime Coaching

RealTime Coaching uses the four principles—that we all have different interests, attitudes and values; that we are motivated by a mismatch between what we want and what we perceive we're getting; that our behavior is our best attempt to correct this mismatch; and that achieving the results we want means changing the want or changing the behavior—as a guide for becoming an effective coach. The best way to begin is to start using these four principles on the job. Start by:

- Observing behavior using the idea of *scales*. Begin identifying what people want and what they perceive they're getting, and assessing whether or not their scales are out of balance.

- Listening for what employees *want* from their jobs, from you, and from others in the organization. They're telling you all the time. Pause and listen.

- Assessing your preferred way of relating on the job: Is it do to, do for, or do with? Self-evaluate the relationships you have with your direct reports, peers, and boss; and commit to changing any relationship you believe can be improved.

- Tightening up your planning. Nothing happens solely with good intentions. They have to be backed up with action.

I hope you're beginning to realize that becoming an effective coach may require you to think quite differently about your management skills and leadership style.

My experience has been that coaching is hard work. Recently, after an afternoon session with a group of senior managers practicing *RealTime Coaching* with role-play cases, I detected a malaise about the group, a certain apathy. I became a bit nervous and asked, "How's everybody doing with *RealTime Coaching?*" The room fell quiet, and finally one of the participants said, "I don't know about the rest of you... but I'm pooped. This is really hard work!"

In listening to many participants beginning to learn *RealTime Coaching*, I usually hear someone say, "It's just really hard to break old habits!" Most managers and executives have a great deal of experience in hierarchical settings where their ability to influence is based on position or title. While the ineffectiveness of this mental model is being realized, the underlying perception of what a boss is may still be quite strong.

As a further aid to helping you break old habits, see Figure 39. I've prepared an outline to help you think through, prepare, and conduct a coaching session.

How Long Does It Take?

I'm often asked, "How long does it take to be a competent *RealTime* coach?" It's a good question. To help you answer it, recall a time you learned a new activity as an adult. Maybe it was tennis, golf, skiing, bridge, or some other sport or game. What determined how long it took you to become as proficient as you are now? I think you'll find it depends on three things:

1. *Desire*—How much do you want to be a proficient, competent, and confident *RealTime* coach? As you look at your current management style and compare it to *RealTime Coaching*, what do you experience? How far out of balance are your scales? If you are not satisfied with where you are, what do you want to do with the energy created?

2. *Study*—Really dig into the concepts presented here.
   Reread Chapters 3–6. You may want to read *Choice Theory*, *The Control Theory Manager*, *The Quality School*, *The Quality School Teacher* or other books by William Glasser. Dr. Glasser has written extensively on what he calls lead-management based on Choice Theory. His writing style is easy to read and jargon free.

3. *Practice*—Reread the cases several times. Have someone play the role of the employee with you as the coach. Read them out loud, together, so you can experience how *RealTime Coaching* just feels different. Then switch roles. You may want to share this book with others in your company. Great learning and understanding can result when groups of people read and talk about the topics presented here. If you have employees you'd like to coach, tell them what you're doing so they won't be threatened. (And don't forget to ask them to self-evaluate how they experienced the coaching session.)

A Challenge

Think for a minute: What would your organization be like if all managers, executives, and leaders committed to practicing the principles of *RealTime Coaching*? What would be the quality of the products produced or services rendered? How would problems be handled? How rapidly could a new procedure be implemented? How many meetings would you have? Would the span of control change? How? How fast could you bring a new product to market? Could anyone compete with you? What would happen to job satisfaction? What would positive change mean to everyone personally?

I urge you to seriously consider this challenge and ask, "Is there really any other way to unleash the power of people?"

Figure 39

Planning a Coaching Session

I. **Background for the Session**
   A. From your (the coach's) point of view:
      1. Where are your scales out of balance?
         a. What do you perceive you're getting or not getting?
         b. What do you want:
            i. for yourself?
            ii. for the employee?
            iii. for others?
            iv. for your organization?
         c. What "values" do you have that are shaping what you perceive you're getting?
      2. What boundaries are being violated?
         a. Interpersonal?
         b. Departmental?
         c. Organizational?
      3. What "hard data" do you have that illustrates what you perceive you're getting?
      4. What are you (or the organization) willing to do to get what you want?
      5. What are the consequences for the employee of not changing?
      6. What would be the characteristics of an acceptable plan?
      7. What are the consequences for the employee of not following through with the plan?
      8. What do you think will be the key points of agreement with the employee?
      9. What do you think will be the key points of disagreement, resistance, or friction with the employee?

   B. With regard to the employee:
1. What behaviors do you observe?
2. Review Chapter 5 and determine the core behavioral style of the person you want to coach.
   a. What are the unique characteristics and potential blindspots of this core behavioral style?
   b. How should you adapt your coaching style based on the tips given for this core behavioral style?
3. What do you think the employee wants?
4. What values may be shaping the employee's perception of what he's getting or not getting?
5. What is effective (or acceptable) or ineffective (or unacceptable) about the employee's performance?

II. Planning for the Session

   A. Complete Background "Section I" above.

   B. What environmental issues need to be addressed?
1. What's the level of trust in the relationship?
   a. if low, should the session take place?
   b. if low, what can be done to increase the level?
2. What do you need to do to maintain an environment conducive to coaching during the session?

   C. Prepare an agenda for the coaching session.
1. What's the single issue you want to focus on?
2. How will you maintain your focus?
3. Where do you want to conduct the session:
   a. your work area?
   b. employee's work area?
   c. other neutral area?
4. What's your entry point?
   a. How will you encourage self-evaluation?
   b. How will you identify wants?

       c. How will you increase self-awareness of behavior?

       d. How will you develop a plan for change?

    5. Estimate a length of time for the session. Can the session be continued?

    6. Set an appointment.

D. Write out:

    1. Three questions that will encourage self-evaluation.

    2. Three questions that will identify wants.

    3. Three questions that will increase self-awareness of total behavior.

    4. Three questions that will develop a plan for change.

III. Conduct Session

IV. Post-session Evaluation

A. What's your overall appraisal of your performance as a coach?

    1. Is what you got what you wanted, or acceptable now?

    2. On a scale of 1 to 10, how would you evaluate your performance as a coach?

B. What did you particularly like about the session?

C. If you had to do it over again, what would you do differently?

Appendix A

Special Note to Appendix A — Please Read

Chapter 3, "What's Your Passion?" discusses a powerful self-assessment profile we use in all of our *RealTime Coaching* workshops. The Personal Interests, Attitudes and Values™ profile helps you understand the values that motivate you. A sample copy of the profile appears in this appendix.

The profile is reproduced here with permission from TTI Performance Systems, Ltd.

If you would like your own personal 35-page profile that includes an analysis of both the values that motivate you and the behaviors you choose to get what you want in life, complete the order form in the back of this book or call Leadership Horizons directly at 1-888-COACH77 (US only, elsewhere 317-844-5587).

PERSONAL INTERESTS, ATTITUDES AND VALUES

*"He who knows others is learned.
He who knows himself is wise."*
–Lao Tse

Jane Doe

Provided by Leadership Horizons creators of RealTime Coaching.

Leadership Horizons, LLC
301 E. Carmel Drive, Suite D 500
Carmel, IN 46032-4812
Telephone toll free 1-888-COACH77 or 317-844-5587
E-Mail: info@leadershiphorizons.com

UNDERSTANDING YOUR REPORT

Knowledge of an individual's attitudes help to tell us WHY they do things. A review of an individual's experiences, references, education and training help to tell us WHAT they can do. Behavioral assessments help to tell us HOW a person behaves and performs in the work environment. The PIAV report measures the relative prominence of six basic interests or attitudes (a way of valuing life): Theoretical, Utilitarian, Aesthetic, Social, Individualistic and Traditional.

Attitudes help to initiate one's behavior and are sometimes called the hidden motivators because they are not always readily observed. It is the purpose of this report to help illuminate and amplify some of those motivating factors and to build on the strengths that each person brings to the work environment.

Based on your choices, this report ranks your relative passion for each of the six attitudes. Your top two and sometimes three attitudes cause you to move into action. You will feel positive when talking, listening or doing activities that satisfy your top attitudes.

The feedback you will receive in this section will reflect one of three intensity levels for each of the six attitudes.

- STRONG - positive feelings that you need to satisfy either on or off the job.

- SITUATIONAL - where your feelings will range from positive to indifferent based on other priorities in your life at the time. These attitudes tend to become more important as your top attitudes are satisfied.

- INDIFFERENT - your feelings will be indifferent when related to your 5th or 6th attitude.

YOUR ATTITUDES RANKING		
1st	UTILITARIAN	Strong
2nd	THEORETICAL	Strong
3rd	INDIVIDUALISTIC	Situational
4th	TRADITIONAL	Situational
5th	AESTHETIC	Indifferent
6th	SOCIAL	Indifferent

Leadership Horizons, LLC
Telephone toll free 1-888-COACH77 or 317-844-5587
E-Mail: info@leadershiphorizons.com

UTILITARIAN

The Utilitarian score shows a characteristic interest in money and what is useful. This means that an individual wants to have the security that money brings not only for themselves, but for their present and future family. This value includes the practical affairs of the business world - the production, marketing and consumption of goods, the use of credit, and the accumulation of tangible wealth. This type of individual is thoroughly practical and conforms well to the stereotype of the average American business person. A person with a high score is likely to have a high need to surpass others in wealth.

- Jane will protect her assets to ensure the future of her economic security.

- Having more wealth than others is a high priority for Jane.

- She can be very practical.

- All attempts are made to protect future security to ensure that her legacy is protected.

- Wealth provides the security Jane wants for herself and her family (if married).

- Jane faces the future confidently.

- Jane will attempt to structure her economic dealings.

- Jane has a long list of wants and will work hard to achieve them.

- With economic security comes the freedom to advance her ideas or beliefs.

- Jane will be motivated by her accomplishments.

- She uses money as a scorecard.

Leadership Horizons, LLC
Telephone toll free 1-888-COACH77 or 317-844-5587
E-Mail: info@leadershiphorizons.com

2

THEORETICAL

The primary drive with this value is the discovery of TRUTH. In pursuit of this value, an individual takes a "cognitive" attitude. Such an individual is nonjudgmental regarding the beauty or utility of objects and seeks only to observe and to reason. Since the interests of the theoretical person are empirical, critical and rational, the person appears to be an intellectual. The chief aim in life is to order and systematize knowledge: knowledge for the sake of knowledge.

- A comfortable job for Jane in one that challenges her knowledge.

- Jane has the potential to become an expert in her chosen field.

- Jane is comfortable around people who share her interest for knowledge and especially those people with similar convictions.

- She will usually have the data to support her convictions.

- Jane is very good at integrating past knowledge to solve present problems.

- She may have difficulty putting down a good book.

Leadership Horizons, LLC
Telephone toll free 1-888-COACH77 or 317-844-5587
E-Mail: info@leadershiphorizons.com

INDIVIDUALISTIC

The primary interest for this value is POWER, not necessarily politics. Research studies indicate that leaders in most fields have a high power value. Since competition and struggle play a large part in all areas of life, many philosophers have seen power as the most universal and most fundamental of motives. There are, however, certain personalities in whom the desire for direct expression of this motive is uppermost; who wish, above all, for personal power, influence and renown.

- She will evaluate each situation individually and determine how much or how little control she will want to exercise.

- Jane can be assertive in meeting her needs.

- At times Jane can be very competitive.

- The amount of control she attempts will increase if she has strong feelings about the issues involved with the situation. If, however, she has little interest in the issues involved, she will not issues see the need for exercising control.

Leadership Horizons, LLC
Telephone toll free 1-888-COACH77 or 317-844-5587
E-Mail: info@leadershiphorizons.com

4

TRADITIONAL

The highest interest for this value may be called "unity," "order," or "tradition." Individuals with high scores in this value seek a system for living. This system can be found in such things as religion, conservatism or any authority that has defined rules, regulations and principles for living.

- Jane needs to be able to pick and choose the traditions and set of beliefs to which she will adhere.

    - Jane at times will evaluate others based on her rules for living.

    - Jane lets her conscience be her guide.

    - She will have strong beliefs within a system that she feels most comfortable with, and she will not be as strong in her beliefs or approach if she lacks that interest level.

Leadership Horizons, LLC
Telephone toll free 1-888-COACH77 or 317-844-5587
E-Mail: info@leadershiphorizons.com

AESTHETIC

A higher Aesthetic score indicates a relative interest in "form and harmony." Each experience is judged from the standpoint of grace, symmetry or fitness. Life may be regarded as a procession of events, and each is enjoyed for its own sake. A high score here does not necessarily mean that the incumbent has talents in creative artistry. It indicates a primary interest in the artistic episodes of life.

- Jane is not necessarily worried about form and beauty in her environment.

- Jane's passion in life will be found in one or two of the other attitudes and values discussed in this report.

- Intellectually, Jane can see the need for beauty, but has difficulty buying the finer things in life.

- The utility of "something" is more important than its beauty, form and harmony.

- Unpleasant surroundings will not stifle her creativity.

- She wants to take a practical approach to events.

- She is a very practical person who is not sensitive to being in harmony with her surroundings.

Leadership Horizons, LLC
Telephone toll free 1-888-COACH77 or 317-844-5587
E-Mail: info@leadershiphorizons.com

6

SOCIAL

Those who score very high in this value have an inherent love of people. The social person prizes other people and is, therefore, kind, sympathetic and unselfish. They are likely to find the Theoretical, Utilitarian and Aesthetic attitudes cold and inhuman. Compared to the Individualistic value, the Social person regards helping others as the only suitable form for human relationships. Research into this value indicates that in its purest form, the Social interest is selfless.

- Jane is willing to help others if they are working as hard as possible to achieve their goals.

- Jane's passion in life will be found in one or two of the other dimensions discussed in this report.

- She will be firm in her decisions and not be swayed by unfortunate circumstances.

- Believing that hard work and persistence is within everyone's reach - she feels things must be earned, not given.

- She will not normally allow herself to be directed by others unless it will enhance her own self-interest.

- Jane will be torn if helping others proves to be detrimental to her.

Leadership Horizons, LLC
Telephone toll free 1-888-COACH77 or 317-844-5587
E-Mail: info@leadershiphorizons.com

ATTITUDES - NORMS & COMPARISONS

For years you have heard statements like, "Different strokes for different folks," "to each his own," and "people do things for their own reasons, not yours." When you are surrounded by people who share similar attitudes, you will fit in with the group and be energized. However, when surrounded by people whose attitudes are significantly different from yours, you may be perceived as out of the mainstream. These differences can induce stress or conflict. When confronted with this type of situation you can:

- Change the situation.
- Change your perception of the situation.
- Leave the situation.
- Cope with the situation.

This section reveals areas where your attitudes may be outside the mainstream and could lead to conflict. The further away you are from the mainstream on the high side, the more people will notice your passion about that attitude. The further away from the mainstream on the low side, the more people will view you as indifferent and possibly negative about that attitude. The shaded area for each attitude represents 68 percent of the population or scores that fall within one standard deviation above or below the national mean.

NORMS & COMPARISONS TABLE		
Jane Doe		
THEORETICAL	*	Mainstream
UTILITARIAN	*	Passionate
AESTHETIC	*	Mainstream
SOCIAL	*	Indifferent
INDIVIDUALISTIC	*	Passionate
TRADITIONAL	*	Indifferent

- 68 percent of the population
| - national mean
* - your score

Mainstream - one standard deviation of the national mean
Passionate - two standard deviations above the national mean
Indifferent - two standard deviations below the national mean
Extreme - three standard deviations from the national mean

Leadership Horizons, LLC
Telephone toll free 1-888-COACH77 or 317-844-5587
E-Mail: info@leadershiphorizons.com

8

ATTITUDES - NORMS & COMPARISONS

Areas in which you have strong feelings or passions compared to others:

- You strive for efficiency and practicality in all areas of your life, seeking to gain a return on your investment of time, talent and resources. Others may feel you always have a string attached and are always trying to gain a personal advantage. They may feel you should give just for the sake of giving.

- You have a strong desire to lead, direct and control your own destiny and the destiny of others. You have a desire to lead and are striving for opportunities to advance your position and influence. Others may believe you are jockeying for position and continually stepping "over the line." They may believe that you form relationships only to "move ahead" and gain an advantage.

Areas where others' strong feelings may frustrate you as you do not share their same passion:

- Your self-reliance will cause you to feel uncomfortable around people who are always trying to help you or be too nice to you.

- Others who try to impose their way of living on you will frustrate you. Your ability to try new things frustrates them and they feel compelled to change you to their system.

Leadership Horizons, LLC
Telephone toll free 1-888-COACH77 or 317-844-5587
E-Mail: info@leadershiphorizons.com

ATTITUDES GRAPH

Jane Doe

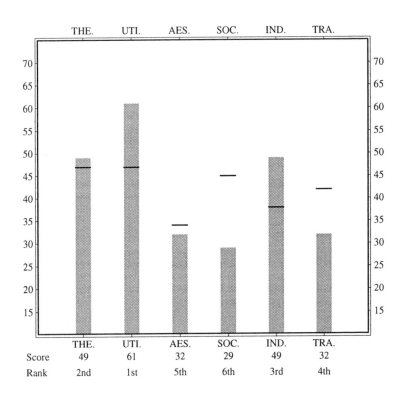

	THE.	UTI.	AES.	SOC.	IND.	TRA.
Score	49	61	32	29	49	32
Rank	2nd	1st	5th	6th	3rd	4th

— national mean

Leadership Horizons, LLC
Telephone toll free 1-888-COACH77 or 317-844-5587
E-Mail: info@leadershiphorizons.com

ATTITUDES WHEEL

Jane Doe

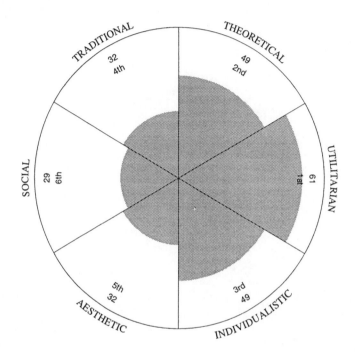

Leadership Horizons, LLC
Telephone toll free 1-888-COACH77 or 317-844-5587
E-Mail: info@leadershiphorizons.com

Appendix B

Special Note to Appendix B — Please Read

Chapter 5, "What Are You Doing?" discusses a powerful self-assessment profile we use in all of our *RealTime Coaching* workshops. The Managing for Success™ profile helps you understand the behavioral style you use to get what you want. The profile has been proven to be accurate across cultures and through decades of use. A sample copy of the Managing for Success™ appears in this appendix.

The profile is reproduced here with permission from TTI Performance Systems, Ltd.

If you would like your own personal 35-page profile that includes an analysis of both the values that motivate you and the behaviors you choose to get what you want in life, complete the order form in the back of this book or call Leadership Horizons directly at 1-888-COACH77 (US only, elsewhere 317-844-5587).

.

MANAGING FOR SUCCESS®

Employee-Manager Version

"He who knows others is learned.
He who knows himself is wise."
–Lao Tse

John Doe

Provided by Leadership Horizons creators of RealTime Coaching.

Leadership Horizons, LLC
301 E. Carmel Drive, Suite D 500
Carmel, IN 46032-4812
Telephone toll free 1-888-COACH77 or 317-844-5587
E-Mail: info@leadershiphorizons.com

Leadership Horizons, LLC
Telephone toll free 1-888-COACH77 or 317-844-5587
E-Mail: info@leadershiphorizons.com

INTRODUCTION

Behavioral research suggests that the most effective people are those who understand themselves, both their strengths and weaknesses, so they can develop strategies to meet the demands of their environment.

A person's behavior is a necessary and integral part of who they are. In other words, much of our behavior comes from "nature" (inherent), and much comes from "nurture" (our upbringing). It is the universal language of "how we act," or our observable human behavior.

In this report we are measuring four dimensions of normal behavior. They are:

- how you respond to problems and challenges.

- how you influence others to your point of view.

- how you respond to the pace of the environment.

- how you respond to rules and procedures set by others.

This report analyzes behavioral style; that is, a person's manner of doing things. Is the report 100% true? Yes, no and maybe. We are only measuring behavior. We only report statements from areas of behavior in which tendencies are shown. To improve accuracy, feel free to make notes or edit the report regarding any statement from the report that may or may not apply, but only after checking with friends or colleagues to see if they agree.

"All people exhibit all four behavioral factors in varying degrees of intensity."
–W.M. Marston

Leadership Horizons, LLC
Telephone toll free 1-888-COACH77 or 317-844-5587
E-Mail: info@leadershiphorizons.com

1

GENERAL CHARACTERISTICS

Based on John's responses, the report has selected general statements to provide a broad understanding of his work style. These statements identify the basic natural behavior that he brings to the job. That is, if left on his own, these statements identify HOW HE WOULD CHOOSE TO DO THE JOB. Use the general characteristics to gain a better understanding of John's natural behavior.

John can be aggressive and direct, but still be considerate of people. Other people realize that directness is one of his great strengths. He is driven toward goals completion and wants to be in a position to set policy that will allow him to meet those goals. He is a self-starter who likes new projects and is most comfortable when involved with a wide scope of activities. He embraces visions not always seen by others. John's creative mind allows him to see the "big picture." John enjoys authority, independence and the freedom that goes with his aggressive approach to problem solving. Most people see him as a high risk-taker. His view is, "nothing ventured, nothing gained." He prefers an environment with variety and change. He is at his best when many projects are underway at once. He likes to be forceful and direct when dealing with others. His desire for results is readily apparent to the people with whom he works. John has high ego strengths and may be viewed by some as egotistical. He wants to be seen as an individual who is totally keyed to results. He wants to get things done in a manner that is consistent with his perception of the "right way" of doing things.

John finds it easy to share his opinions on solving work-related problems. Sometimes he becomes emotionally involved in the decision-making process. He prefers authority equal to his responsibility. He is decisive and prefers to work for a decisive manager. He can experience stress if his manager does not possess similar traits. When faced with a tough decision, he will try to sell you on his ideas. He should realize that at times he needs to think

Leadership Horizons, LLC
Telephone toll free 1-888-COACH77 or 317-844-5587
E-Mail: info@leadershiphorizons.com

2

GENERAL CHARACTERISTICS

a project through, beginning to end, before starting the project. He has the unique ability of tackling tough problems and following them through to a satisfactory conclusion. He will work long hours until a tough problem is solved. After it is solved, John may become bored with any routine work that follows.

John should exhibit more patience and ask questions to make sure that others have understood what he has said. He tends to be intolerant of people who seem ambiguous or think too slowly. He may lose interest in what others are saying if they ramble or don't speak to the point. His active mind is already moving ahead. His creative and active mind may hinder his ability to communicate to others effectively. He may present the information in a form that cannot be easily understood by some people. John challenges people who volunteer their opinions. He may lack the patience to listen and communicate with slower acting people. He may sometimes mask his feelings in friendly terms. If pressured, John's true feelings may emerge. He tends to influence people by being direct, friendly and results-oriented.

Leadership Horizons, LLC
Telephone toll free 1-888-COACH77 or 317-844-5587
E-Mail: info@leadershiphorizons.com

VALUE TO THE ORGANIZATION

This section of the report identifies the specific talents and behavior John brings to the job. By looking at these statements, one can identify his role in the organization. The organization can then develop a system to capitalize on his particular value and make him an integral part of the team.

- Challenge-oriented.

- Self-starter.

- Creative in his approach to solving problems.

- Tenacious.

- Thinks big.

- Positive sense of humor.

- Optimistic and enthusiastic.

- Forward-looking and future-oriented.

Leadership Horizons, LLC
Telephone toll free 1-888-COACH77 or 317-844-5587
E-Mail: info@leadershiphorizons.com

4

CHECKLIST FOR COMMUNICATING

Most people are aware of and sensitive to the ways with which they prefer to be communicated. Many people find this section to be extremely accurate and important for enhanced interpersonal communication. This page provides other people with a list of things to DO when communicating with John. Read each statement and identify the 3 or 4 statements which are most important to him. We recommend highlighting the most important "DO's" and provide a listing to those who communicate with John most frequently.

Do:

- Provide questions, alternatives and choices for making his own decisions.

- Offer special, immediate and continuing incentives for his willingness to take risks.

- Talk about him, his goals and the opinions he finds stimulating.

- Be clear, specific, brief and to the point.

- Read the body language--look for impatience or disapproval.

- Provide facts and figures about probability of success, or effectiveness of options.

- Provide a warm and friendly environment.

- Ask for his opinions/ideas regarding people.

- Support the results, not the person, if you agree.

- Leave time for relating, socializing.

- Motivate and persuade by referring to objectives and results.

- Provide ideas for implementing action.

- Plan interaction that supports his dreams and intentions.

Leadership Horizons, LLC
Telephone toll free 1-888-COACH77 or 317-844-5587
E-Mail: info@leadershiphorizons.com

DON'TS ON COMMUNICATING

This section of the report is a list of things NOT to do while communicating with John. Review each statement with John and identify those methods of communication that result in frustration or reduced performance. By sharing this information, both parties can negotiate a communication system that is mutually agreeable.

Don't:

- Let disagreement reflect on him personally.

- Drive on to facts, figures, alternatives or abstractions.

- Waste time trying to be impersonal, judgmental or too task-oriented.

- "Dream" with him or you'll lose time.

- Try to convince by "personal" means.

- Ramble on, or waste his time.

- Take credit for his ideas.

- Leave decisions hanging in the air.

- Come with a ready-made decision, or make it for him.

- Direct or order.

- Ask rhetorical questions, or useless ones.

- Talk down to him.

- Try to build personal relationships.

Leadership Horizons, LLC
Telephone toll free 1-888-COACH77 or 317-844-5587
E-Mail: info@leadershiphorizons.com

6

COMMUNICATION TIPS

This section provides suggestions on methods which will improve John's communications with others. The tips include a brief description of typical people in which he may interact. By adapting to the communication style desired by other people, John will become more effective in his communications with them. He may have to practice some flexibility in varying his communication style with others who may be different from himself. This flexibility and the ability to interpret the needs of others is the mark of a superior communicator.

When communicating with a person who is ambitious, forceful, decisive, strong-willed, independent and goal-oriented:

- Be clear, specific, brief and to the point.

- Stick to business.

- Be prepared with support material in a well-organized "package."

Factors that will create tension or dissatisfaction:

- Talking about things that are not relevant to the issue.

- Leaving loopholes or cloudy issues.

- Appearing disorganized.

When communicating with a person who is magnetic, enthusiastic, friendly, demonstrative and political:

- Provide a warm and friendly environment.

- Don't deal with a lot of details (put them in writing).

- Ask "feeling" questions to draw their opinions or comments.

Factors that will create tension or dissatisfaction:

- Being curt, cold or tight-lipped.

- Controlling the conversation.

- Driving on facts and figures, alternatives, abstractions.

Leadership Horizons, LLC
Telephone toll free 1-888-COACH77 or 317-844-5587
E-Mail: info@leadershiphorizons.com

COMMUNICATION TIPS

When communicating with a person who is patient, predictable, reliable, steady, relaxed and modest:

- Begin with a personal comment--break the ice.

- Present your case softly, nonthreateningly.

- Ask "how?" questions to draw their opinions.

Factors that will create tension or dissatisfaction:

- Rushing headlong into business.

- Being domineering or demanding.

- Forcing them to respond quickly to your objectives.

When communicating with a person who is dependent, neat, conservative, perfectionist, careful and compliant:

- Prepare your "case" in advance.

- Stick to business.

- Be accurate and realistic.

Factors that will create tension or dissatisfaction:

- Being giddy, casual, informal, loud.

- Pushing too hard or being unrealistic with deadlines.

- Being disorganized or messy.

Leadership Horizons, LLC
Telephone toll free 1-888-COACH77 or 317-844-5587
E-Mail: info@leadershiphorizons.com

8

IDEAL ENVIRONMENT

This section identifies the ideal work environment based on John's basic style. People with limited flexibility will find themselves uncomfortable working in any job not described in this section. People with flexibility use intelligence to modify their behavior and can be comfortable in many environments. Use this section to identify specific duties and responsibilities that John enjoys and also those that create frustration.

- Nonroutine work with challenge and opportunity.

- valuation based on results, not the process.

- Freedom of movement.

- Forum to express ideas and viewpoints.

- An innovative and futuristic-oriented environment.

- Work tasks that change from time to time.

- Assignments with a high degree of people contacts.

- Democratic supervisor with whom he can associate.

Leadership Horizons, LLC
Telephone toll free 1-888-COACH77 or 317-844-5587
E-Mail: info@leadershiphorizons.com

PERCEPTIONS

A person's behavior and feelings may be quickly telegraphed to others. This section provides additional information on John's self-perception and how, under certain conditions, others may perceive his behavior. Understanding this section will empower John to project the image that will allow him to control the situation.

"See Yourself As Others See You"

SELF-PERCEPTION

John usually sees himself as being:

Pioneering	Assertive
Competitive	Confident
Positive	Winner

OTHERS' PERCEPTION

Under moderate pressure, tension, stress or fatigue, others may see him as being:

Demanding	Nervy
Egotistical	Aggressive

And, under extreme pressure, stress or fatigue, others may see him as being:

Abrasive	Controlling
Arbitrary	Opinionated

DESCRIPTORS

Based on John's responses, the report has marked those words that describe his personal behavior. They describe how he solves problems and meets challenges, influences people, responds to the pace of the environment and how he responds to rules and procedures set by others.

Dominance	Influencing	Steadiness	Compliance
Demanding	Effusive	Phlegmatic	Evasive
Egocentric	Inspiring	Relaxed	Worrisome
		Resistant to Change	Careful
Driving	Magnetic	Nondemonstrative	Dependent
Ambitious	Political		Cautious
Pioneering	Enthusiastic	Passive	Conventional
Strong-Willed	Demonstrative		Exacting
Forceful	Persuasive	Patient	Neat
Determined	Warm		
Aggressive	Convincing	Possessive	Systematic
Competitive	Polished		Diplomatic
Decisive	Poised	Predictable	Accurate
Venturesome	Optimistic	Consistent	Tactful
		Deliberate	
Inquisitive	Trusting	Steady	Open-Minded
Responsible	Sociable	Stable	Balanced Judgment
Conservative	Reflective	Mobile	Firm
Calculating	Factual	Active	Independent
Cooperative	Calculating	Restless	Self-Willed
Hesitant	Skeptical	Alert	Stubborn
Low-Keyed		Variety-Oriented	
Unsure	Logical	Demonstrative	
Undemanding	Undemonstrative		Obstinate
Cautious	Suspicious	Impatient	Opinionated
	Matter-of-Fact	Pressure-Oriented	Unsystematic
Mild	Incisive	Eager	Self-Righteous
Agreeable		Flexible	Uninhibited
Modest	Pessimistic	Impulsive	Arbitrary
Peaceful	Moody	Impetuous	Unbending
Unobtrusive	Critical	Hypertense	Careless with Details

Leadership Horizons, LLC
Telephone toll free 1-888-COACH77 or 317-844-5587
E-Mail: info@leadershiphorizons.com

NATURAL AND ADAPTED STYLE

John's natural style of dealing with problems, people, pace of events and procedures may not always fit what the environment needs. This section will provide valuable information related to stress and the pressure to adapt to the environment.

PROBLEMS - CHALLENGES (Natural)

John tends to deal with problems and challenges in a demanding, driving and self-willed manner. He is individualistic in his approach and actively seeks goals. John will attack problems and likes a position with authority and work that will constantly challenge him to perform up to his ability.

PROBLEMS - CHALLENGES (Adapted)

John's response to the environment is to be strong-willed and ambitious in his problem-solving approach. He seeks to win against all obstacles.

PEOPLE - CONTACTS (Natural)

John is enthusiastic about his ability to influence others. He prefers an environment in which he has the opportunity to deal with different types of individuals. John is trusting and also wants to be trusted.

PEOPLE - CONTACTS (Adapted)

John sees no need to change his approach to influencing others to his way of thinking. He sees his natural style to be what the environment is calling for.

Leadership Horizons, LLC
Telephone toll free 1-888-COACH77 or 317-844-5587
E-Mail: info@leadershiphorizons.com

12

NATURAL AND ADAPTED STYLE

PACE - CONSISTENCY (Natural)

John is variety-oriented and demonstrates a need to get from one activity to another as quickly as possible. He usually demonstrates a pronounced sense of urgency. He is eager to initiate change if for nothing else than for change's sake.

PACE - CONSISTENCY (Adapted)

John sees his natural activity style to be just what the environment needs. What you see is what you get for activity level and consistency. Sometimes he would like the world to slow down.

PROCEDURES - CONSTRAINTS (Natural)

John is independent by nature and feels comfortable in situations where the constraints are few and far between. He will follow rules as long as he feels that the rules are his. He has a tendency to rebel from rules set by others and wants input into any constraints.

PROCEDURES - CONSTRAINTS (Adapted)

John shows little discomfort when comparing his basic (natural) style to his response to the environment (adapted) style. The difference is not significant and John sees little or no need to change his response to the environment.

Leadership Horizons, LLC
Telephone toll free 1-888-COACH77 or 317-844-5587
E-Mail: info@leadershiphorizons.com

ADAPTED STYLE

John sees his present work environment requiring him to exhibit the behavior listed on this page. If the following statements DO NOT sound job related, explore the reasons why he is adapting this behavior.

- Meeting deadlines.

- Skillful use of vocabulary for persuasive situations.

- Persistence in job completion.

- Anticipating and solving problems.

- Handling a variety of activities.

- Acting without precedent, and able to respond to change in daily work.

- Moving quickly from one activity to another.

- A good support team to handle paperwork.

- Working without close supervision.

- Exhibiting an active and creative sense of humor.

- Questioning the status quo, and seeking more effective ways of accomplishment.

Leadership Horizons, LLC
Telephone toll free 1-888-COACH77 or 317-844-5587
E-Mail: info@leadershiphorizons.com

14

KEYS TO MOTIVATING

This section of the report was produced by analyzing John's wants. People are motivated by the things they want; thus wants that are satisfied no longer motivate. Review each statement produced in this section with John and highlight those that are present "wants."

John wants:

- Freedom from routine work.

- Power and authority to take the risks to achieve results.

- Changing environments in which to work/play.

- Outside activities so there is never a dull moment.

- More time in the day.

- New challenges and problems to solve.

- To be seen as a leader.

- A wide scope of activities.

- Support system to help with details and follow through.

- Prestige, position and titles so he can control the destiny of others.

- Travel or changing work stations.

Leadership Horizons, LLC
Telephone toll free 1-888-COACH77 or 317-844-5587
E-Mail: info@leadershiphorizons.com

KEYS TO MANAGING

In this section are some needs which must be met in order for John to perform at an optimum level. Some needs can be met by himself, while management must provide for others. It is difficult for a person to enter a motivational environment when that person's basic management needs have not been fulfilled. Review the list with John and identify 3 or 4 statements that are most important to him. This allows John to participate in forming his own personal management plan.

John needs:

- More logical presentations--less emotional.

- To handle routine paperwork only once.

- To mask emotions when appropriate.

- To be confronted when in disagreement, or when he breaks the rules.

- To focus conversations on work activities--less socializing.

- A program for pacing work and relaxing.

- To negotiate commitment face-to-face.

- To maintain focus on results and not sacrifice productivity just to make everyone happy.

- Help on controlling time and setting priorities.

- To understand his role on the team--either a team player or the leader.

- Participatory management.

- More control of body language.

Leadership Horizons, LLC
Telephone toll free 1-888-COACH77 or 317-844-5587
E-Mail: info@leadershiphorizons.com

16

AREAS FOR IMPROVEMENT

In this area is a listing of possible limitations without regard to a specific job. Review with John and cross out those limitations that do not apply. Highlight 1 to 3 limitations that are hindering his performance and develop an action plan to eliminate or reduce this hindrance.

John has a tendency to:

- Be disruptive because of his innate restlessness and disdain for sameness.

- Make "off the cuff" remarks that are often seen as personal prods.

- Be impulsive and seek change for change's sake. May change priorities daily.

- Be a one-way communicator--doesn't listen to the total story before introducing his opinion.

- Be inconsistent because of many stops, starts and ever-changing direction.

- Resist participation as part of the team, unless seen as a leader.

- Fail to complete what he starts because of adding more and more projects.

- Have no concept of the problems that slower-moving people may have with his style.

Leadership Horizons, LLC
Telephone toll free 1-888-COACH77 or 317-844-5587
E-Mail: info@leadershiphorizons.com

ACTION PLAN

Name: John Doe

The following are examples of areas in which John may want to improve. Circle 1 to 3 areas and develop action plan(s) to bring about the desired results. Look over the report for possible areas that need improvement.

Communicating (Listening)   Time Management
Delegating   Career Goals
Decision Making   Personal Goals
Disciplining   Motivating Others
Evaluating Performance   Developing People
Education   Family

Area:

1.

2.

3.

Area:

1.

2.

3.

Area:

1.

2.

3.

Date to Begin: _____ Date to Review: _____

Leadership Horizons, LLC
Telephone toll free 1-888-COACH77 or 317-844-5587
E-Mail: info@leadershiphorizons.com

BEHAVIORAL FACTOR INDICATOR™

Management Version

John Doe

Provided by Leadership Horizons creators of RealTime Coaching

Leadership Horizons, LLC
959 Keystone Way
Carmel, IN 46032-2823
Telephone toll free 1-888-COACH77 or 317-844-5587
E-Mail: info@leadershiphorizons.com

Leadership Horizons, LLC
Telephone toll free 1-888-COACH77 or 317-844-5587
E-Mail: info@leadershiphorizons.com

INTRODUCTION

Classifying management behavior is not an easy undertaking, largely because there are so many variables on which classifications could be based. The classifications in this report are purely behavioral. Behavioral measurement can be classified as how a person will do a job. No consideration has been given to age, experience, training or values.

Your report will graphically display your behavioral skills in 12 specific factors. Each factor was carefully selected allowing anyone to be successful if they meet the behavioral demands of the job.

The Natural graph represents your natural behavior - the behavior you bring to the job. The Adapted graph measures your response to the environment - the behavior you think is necessary to succeed at a job. If your Adapted graph is significantly different from your Natural, you are under pressure to change or "mask" your behavior.

Read and compare your graphs. Look at each factor and the importance of that factor to the successful performance of your job. Your Adapted graph will identify the factors you see as important and shows you where you are focusing your energy.
Knowledge of your behavior will allow you to develop strategies to win in any environment you choose.

Leadership Horizons, LLC
Telephone toll free 1-888-COACH77 or 317-844-5587
E-Mail: info@leadershiphorizons.com

SPECIFIC FACTOR ANALYSIS

John Doe

DECISIVENESS/RESULTS ORIENTED
```
0...1...2...3...4...5...6...7...8...9...10
```
Natural   9.00
Adapted   8.75

SENSE OF URGENCY
```
0...1...2...3...4...5...6...7...8...9...10
```
Natural   9.00
Adapted   9.25

VISION FOR THE FUTURE
```
0...1...2...3...4...5...6...7...8...9...10
```
Natural   9.75
Adapted   9.50

MOTIVATING OTHERS
```
0...1...2...3...4...5...6...7...8...9...10
```
Natural   9.25
Adapted   9.75

SELF-CONFIDENCE
```
0...1...2...3...4...5...6...7...8...9...10
```
Natural   8.25
Adapted   8.25

CUSTOMER/EMPLOYEE INTERFACE
```
0...1...2...3...4...5...6...7...8...9...10
```
Natural   7.50
Adapted   6.75

Leadership Horizons, LLC
Telephone toll free 1-888-COACH77 or 317-844-5587
E-Mail: info@leadershiphorizons.com

SPECIFIC FACTOR ANALYSIS

John Doe

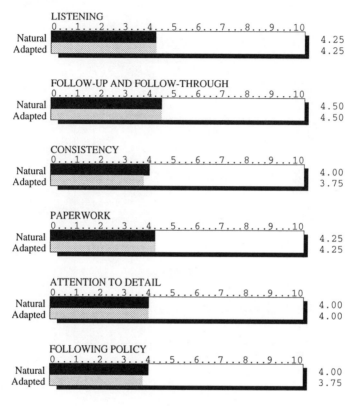

LISTENING
```
         0...1...2...3...4...5...6...7...8...9...10
Natural                                                      4.25
Adapted                                                      4.25
```

FOLLOW-UP AND FOLLOW-THROUGH
```
         0...1...2...3...4...5...6...7...8...9...10
Natural                                                      4.50
Adapted                                                      4.50
```

CONSISTENCY
```
         0...1...2...3...4...5...6...7...8...9...10
Natural                                                      4.00
Adapted                                                      3.75
```

PAPERWORK
```
         0...1...2...3...4...5...6...7...8...9...10
Natural                                                      4.25
Adapted                                                      4.25
```

ATTENTION TO DETAIL
```
         0...1...2...3...4...5...6...7...8...9...10
Natural                                                      4.00
Adapted                                                      4.00
```

FOLLOWING POLICY
```
         0...1...2...3...4...5...6...7...8...9...10
Natural                                                      4.00
Adapted                                                      3.75
```

Leadership Horizons, LLC
Telephone toll free 1-888-COACH77 or 317-844-5587
E-Mail: info@leadershiphorizons.com

STYLE ANALYSIS GRAPHS

John Doe

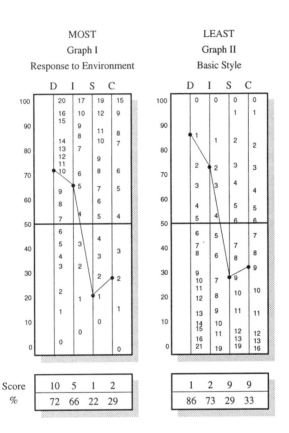

	MOST					LEAST			
	Graph I					Graph II			
	Response to Environment					Basic Style			

Score 10 5 1 2   1 2 9 9

% 72 66 22 29   86 73 29 33

Leadership Horizons, LLC
Telephone toll free 1-888-COACH77 or 317-844-5587
E-Mail: info@leadershiphorizons.com

THE SUCCESS INSIGHTS WHEEL™

INTRODUCTION

The Success Insights Wheel™ is a powerful tool popularized in Europe. In addition to the text you have received about your behavioral style, the Wheel adds a visual representation that allows you to:

• View your natural behavioral style (circle).

• View your adapted behavioral style (star).

• Note the degree you are adapting your behavior.

• If you filled out the Work Environment Analysis, view the relationship of your behavior to your job.

Notice on the next page that your Natural style (circle) and your Adapted style (star) are plotted on the Wheel. If they are plotted in different boxes, then you are adapting your behavior. The further the two plotting points are from each other, the more you are adapting your behavior.

If you are part of a group or team who also took the DISC behavioral assessment, it would be advantageous to get together, using each person's Wheel, and make a master Wheel that contains each person's Natural and Adapted style. This allows you to quickly see where conflict can occur. You will also be able to identify where communication, understanding and appreciation can be increased.

Leadership Horizons, LLC
Telephone toll free 1-888-COACH77 or 317-844-5587
E-Mail: info@leadershiphorizons.com

Copyright © 1984-1998. Target Training International, Ltd.

23

THE SUCCESS INSIGHTS WHEEL™

John Doe

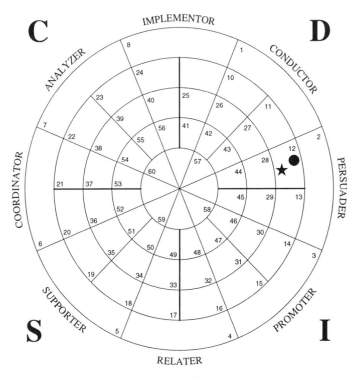

Adapted: ★ (12) CONDUCTING PERSUADER
Natural: ● (12) CONDUCTING PERSUADER

Leadership Horizons, LLC
Telephone toll free 1-888-COACH77 or 317-844-5587
E-Mail: info@leadershiphorizons.com

Additional Readings

Argyris, C. *Reasoning, Learning and Action: Individual and Organizational*. San Francisco: Jossey-Bass, 1982.

Block, P. *Flawless Consulting: A Guide to Getting Your Expertise Used*. Austin: Learning Concepts, 1981.

Bonnstetter, B. J., J. I. Suiter, and R. J. Widrick. *The Universal Language DISC: A Reference Manual*. Scottsdale, AZ: Target Training International, Ltd., 1993.

Bonnstetter, B. J., J. I Suiter, and R. J. Widrick. *Personal Interests, Attitudes, and Values: Study Guide for Certification*. Scottsdale, AZ: Target Training International, Ltd., 1996.

Bonnstetter, B. J., J. I Suiter, and R. J. Widrick. *Style Analysis: Study Guide for Certification*. Scottsdale, AZ: Target Training International, Ltd., 1996.

Conger, J. *Learning to Lead: The Art of Transforming Managers into Leaders*. San Francisco: Jossey-Bass, 1992.

Covey, S. *The Seven Habits of Highly Effective People*. New York: Fireside, Simon & Shuster, 1989.

Fritz, R. *The Path of Least Resistance: Learning to Become the Creative Force in Your Own Life*. New York: Fawcett Columbine, 1989.

Gabor, A. *The Man Who Discovered Quality: How W. Edwards Deming Brought the Quality Revolution to America - The Stories of Ford, Xerox, and GM*. New York: Random House, 1990.

Glasser, W. *Choice Theory: A New Psychology of Personal Freedom*. New York: Harper Collins, 1998.

Glasser, W. *Control Theory: A New Explanation of How We Control Our Lives*. New York: Harper & Row, 1984.

Glasser, W. *The Control Theory Manager*. New York: Harper Business, 1994.

Goldberg, M. *The Art of the Question*. New York: John Wiley & Sons, Inc., 1998.

Gordon, T. *Leader Effectiveness Training, L. E. T., The No-Lose Way To Release the Productive Potential of People*. New York: Bantam Books, 1977.

Mager, R. *Goal Analysis*. Belmont, CA: Lake Publishing Company, 1984.

Miller, S., D. Wackman, E. Nunnally, and C. Saline. *Straight Talk: A New Way To Get Closer to Others by Saying What You Really Mean*. New York: Signet, 1982.

Senge, P., C. Roberts, R. B. Ross, B. J. Smith, A. Kleiner. *The Fifth Discipline Fieldbook: Strategies and Tools for Building a Learning Organization*. New York: Currency Doubleday, 1994.

Shapiro, E. *Fad Surfing in the Boardroom; Reclaiming the Courage to Manage in the Age of Instant Answers*. Reading, MA: Addison-Wesley, 1995.

Walter, J. and J. Peller. *Becoming Solution-Focused in Brief Therapy*. New York: Brunner/Mazel, 1992.

Whitney, J. *The Economics of Trust: Liberating Profits & Restoring Corporate Vitality*. New York: McGraw-Hill, 1996.

Wubbolding, R. *Using Reality Therapy*. New York: Harper & Row, 1988.

Wubbolding, R. *Employee Motivation*. Knoxville: SPC, Inc., 1995.

About the Author

Ron Ernst is president of Leadership Horizons, LLC, a firm that specializes in leadership coaching, executive assessment, and strategy implementation.

Prior to establishing his own consulting practice in 1983, Ron was an executive vice president with Management Horizons, now a division of Price-Waterhouse. From 1990-1994, Ron was an independent affiliate consultant with the Covey Leadership Center, where he worked with organizations implementing principle-centered cultures based on the book *The Seven Habits of Highly Effective People*.

Ron has taught in the MBA program at Indiana University and Capitol University (Columbus, OH), and the undergraduate program at Franklin University (Columbus, OH).

Ron holds a BS in Marketing from Indiana University and an MBA in manpower and industrial relations from The Ohio State University. He is Reality Therapy Certified by The William Glasser Institute. Ron is also a Certified Professional Behavioral Analyst and Certified Professional Values Analyst. Both certifications are from TTI Performance Systems, Ltd.

Leadership Horizons, LLC

Leadership Horizons' goal is to provide our clients the tools to improve their effectiveness on the job as it relates to getting things done with and through other people.

RealTime Coaching
A video-assisted coach training program available to companies, organizations, and institutions.

Personal Insights Workshop
Introductory workshop using self-assessment profiles for improved executive effectiveness.

RealTime Coaching 360° Feedback Profile

Provides feedback to coach, based on the *RealTime Coaching* model. Includes nine profiles; 1 self, 1 boss, and 7 peer and/or direct report.

Contact us for more information on our public enrollment programs, our on-site train-the-trainer programs, and our "teleclass" training by telephone.

If you are a training or consulting organization and would like to know more about becoming a certified *RealTime Coaching* training site, please contact us.

For more information, contact:

Ron Ernst
President
301 E. Carmel Drive, Suite D 500 • Carmel, IN 46032-481?
(317) 844-5587 • Toll free 1-888-COACH77
http://www.leadershiphorizons.com
ron@leadershiphorizons.com

RealTime
Coaching

RealTime Coaching by Ron Ernst	US $24.95	_____
	Canada $29.95	_____
Personal Values and Behavioral Style Profile	US $149.00	_____
	Canada $169.00	_____

Includes two self-administered profiles,
Personal Interests, Attitudes and Values™ and
Managing for Success™. Requires IBM compatible
PC, 3.5" disc drive and Windows 95 or later

Subtotal	_____
US Sales Tax: Please add 5% *(IN residents only)*	Tax	_____
Canada add GST 7% + 8% PST*(in Ontario)*		
Shipping: $5.00 for the first item and $3.00 for each additional item	Shipping	_____
Total	_____

Payment:

_____ Check

_____ Credit Card *(please circle one)*

US- MasterCard VISA AMERICAN EXPRESS

Canada- VISA

Card number_____

Name on Card_____Exp. Date_____

Signature_____

Total amount enclosed:_____

Mail To:

Name _____

Mailing Address_____

_____

City, State, Zip_____

Daytime Telephone_____

IN US ORDER:
Leadership Horizons, LLC
301 E. Carmel Drive, Suite D 500
Carmel, IN 46032-4812

Toll Free 1-888-262-2477
Fax (317) 581-9226
info@leadershiphorizons.com

IN CANADA ORDER:
Excel Group Development
110 Eglinton Ave. E. Suite #703
Toronto, Ontario M4P-241
Canada

Toll free 1-888-89COACH
info@excelgroupdev.com

RealTime Coaching

RealTime Coaching by Ron Ernst	US $24.95	_____
	Canada $29.95	_____
Personal Values and Behavioral Style Profile	US $149.00	_____
	Canada $169.00	_____

Includes two self-administered profiles,
Personal Interests, Attitudes and Values™ and
Managing for Success™. Requires IBM compatible
PC, 3.5" disc drive and Windows 95 or later

	Subtotal	_____
US Sales Tax: Please add 5% *(IN residents only)*	Tax	_____
Canada add GST 7% + 8% PST*(in Ontario)*		
Shipping: $5.00 for the first item and	Shipping	_____
$3.00 for each additional item		
	Total	_____

Payment:

_____ Check   US- MasterCard VISA AMERICAN EXPRESS

_____ Credit Card *(please circle one)*   Canada- VISA

Card number_____

Name on Card_____Exp. Date_____

Signature_____

Total amount enclosed:_____

Mail To:

Name _____

Mailing Address_____

_____

City, State, Zip_____

Daytime Telephone_____

IN US ORDER:
Leadership Horizons, LLC
301 E. Carmel Drive, Suite D 500
Carmel, IN 46032-4812

Toll Free 1-888-262-2477
Fax (317) 581-9226
info@leadershiphorizons.com

IN CANADA ORDER:
Excel Group Development
110 Eglinton Ave. E. Suite #703
Toronto, Ontario M4P-241
Canada

Toll free 1-888-89COACH
info@excelgroupdev.com

RealTime Coaching

RealTime Coaching by Ron Ernst	US $24.95	_____
	Canada $29.95	_____
Personal Values and Behavioral Style Profile	US $149.00	_____
	Canada $169.00	_____

Includes two self-administered profiles, Personal Interests, Attitudes and Values™ and Managing for Success™. Requires IBM compatible PC, 3.5" disc drive and Windows 95 or later

	Subtotal	_____

US Sales Tax: Please add 5% *(IN residents only)*   Tax _____
Canada add GST 7% + 8% PST*(in Ontario)*

Shipping: $5.00 for the first item and   Shipping _____
$3.00 for each additional item

Total _____

Payment:

_____ Check   US- MasterCard VISA AMERICAN EXPRESS

_____ Credit Card *(please circle one)*   Canada- VISA

Card number_____

Name on Card_____Exp. Date_____

Signature_____

Total amount enclosed:_____

Mail To:

Name _____

Mailing Address_____

_____

City, State, Zip_____

Daytime Telephone_____

IN US ORDER:
Leadership Horizons, LLC
301 E. Carmel Drive, Suite D 500
Carmel, IN 46032-4812

Toll Free 1-888-262-2477
Fax (317) 581-9226
info@leadershiphorizons.com

IN CANADA ORDER:
Excel Group Development
110 Eglinton Ave. E. Suite #703
Toronto, Ontario M4P-241
Canada

Toll free 1-888-89COACH
info@excelgroupdev.com